CW00449172

Introduction

I wanted to write a book on what managers need to know in order to help them become more effective. There are many books about management and, in this respect, I felt rather like Elizabeth Taylor's eighth husband on his wedding night – knowing what to do but not being exactly sure how to do it!

I decided, therefore, to write in a manner, which is audaciously simple and seemingly superficial. In this way, it would be easy to read and still have all the salient points concisely and clearly set out. It takes courage to keep things simple, especially in an academic environment, but, in the philosophy I am expounding in this book, there are only a few things a good manager needs to know but he needs to know and understand them well.

20% of what we do governs 80% of our success – this book is about that 20%.

PUBLISHED BY:
THOMAS R DIXON & COMPANY
Bermuda House,
1A Dinsdale Place,
Sandyford
Newcastle upon Tyne
NE2 1BD

Telephone: 0191 2322628

Copyright Reserved.

ISBNs:
Paperback: 978-1-80227-131-7
ebook: 978-1-80227-132-4

The effective executive and time management

Management Self Development

A great many people are in high management positions without ever having been trained in the subject of management. Certainly they have qualifications but these do not necessarily mean they can manage professionally. Once they have acquired their necessary abilities, what managers need most are the skills of dealing with people, of teamwork and of handling information. In more detail, these are the skills of leadership and motivation: team building: staff recruitment, training, counselling and appraisal: listening: delegation and, above all, the ability to develop these skills on others. The management skills they need are those of setting objectives, making decisions, planning and controlling, solving problems, communicating and the ability to analyse past successes and failures. With these skills and this approach managers can plan and improve future performance.

But before all of this, managers most need SELF ANALYSIS and SELF DEVELOPMENT.

They cannot hope to manage others unless they can first manage themselves. Industry, ability, intelligence, imagination and knowledge are all wasted without the skills to convert them into results.

Too many executives do not take responsibility for their own managerial development. They lie back and let their company make the pace and their SUCCESS/POWER lies like an untapped oil field.

Experience in the United States shows the opposite situation. The responsibility is very definitely that of the manager who researches, plans and seeks out every opportunity for wider knowledge and career development. The manager is thus able to realise their true potential and accomplish what others might not achieve in half a dozen lifetimes.

Like an iceberg, is most of your management potential and success power under the surface?

1

We need executive productivity

It is sad that we do not put people into accounting statements and give them an economic value to the most precious resource in any organisation – its human assets. Perhaps, if we did, we would place a far greater value on people, exploit their ability and talent better and make them more accountable for their performance and achievement.

Unquestionably, the success of an enterprise is directly related to the efficiency and effectiveness of its top people – the executives and managers – and this is reflected in ability and a high return on the capital invested. Winning companies highly compensate and place a great value on effective top people. If managers and executives are ineffectual, it permeates through the whole organisation and, like a contagious disease, is caught by the people working below them.

But many companies are still getting it all wrong! They have work-studied their offices, the shop and factory floors, their transport and distribution systems but, only a few have actually undertaken a systematic work-study of their top directors and managers. Yet this is a high priority area where a close study could produce a very high payback.

The message coming back from work-studies of company directors and managers, professional people such as lawyers, doctors, academics, civil servants and government administrators is that few of them are REALLY effective. The average performance seems to be just that – average.

Good managers appear to be scarce. Sometimes like only 10% of managers seems to have the necessary qualities for effectiveness.

Only by developing good management skills can we ever hope to succeed in increasing our achievements, productivity and wealth, enhancing our job satisfaction and creating a happier life style.

Self appraisal takes courage

Have you recently questioned your own:
PERSONAL PRODUCTIVITY

PERFORMANCE
ACHIEVEMENTS
JOB SATISFACTION

If not, you may be getting into a rut and the only difference between a rut and a grave is the depth. Many management people are blind and deaf to their own ineffectiveness and are so embroiled in their daily activities that they fail to regularly re-appraise and evaluate their own work and life performance. Yet a systematic study practised with objectivity and strong self-discipline, can lead to the most rewarding and meaningful results.

The old Greek adage, "know thyself", takes on a real significance in the world of management. Self-knowledge is the result of a candid and sometimes painful appraisal of personal qualities and it is a discipline, which can convert inherent weaknesses into strengths. All of us have a self-deception facility so we need to re-appraise our performance regularly to improve. Sir Walter Scott said, "O, what a tangled web we weave, when first we practise to deceive".

Search for the truth by penetratingly questioning your habits, your self-deceptions – both within and without -, your prejudices and your stale dogmas, all of which can blind you to reality. In 1917, the Russian Tsar ignored the obvious signs of revolution and reassured himself by concentrating on trivia. How wonderful the power of self-deception.

To be yourself and to know yourself calls for a daily review of your conduct under the stresses and tensions of your daily business and social life.

There is a need for all of us to regularly put the two most important things managers should have on their desks – their feet (THINKING TIME) and we should be carefully STOPPING, LOOKING AND LISTENING and systematically considering a radical appraisal of personal effectiveness and accomplishments.

Start by asking:

What are you? What is the main purpose of your job?
Are you acting and meeting targets?
What are your strengths? Are you exploiting them?
What are your weaknesses? Are you putting them right?
What are you NOT DOING that you should be?
What should you stop doing?
Are you achieving success in your work and improving your quality of life?

Some call this 'helicopter' management where one hovers and looks down to get life and work into perspective.

A story that illustrates the need to question our beliefs concerns an Irish/Jewish Catholic priest named Zolly Murphyberg who died and went to heaven. But, when he got there, God told him that he was too early and sent him back to earth. This was the first time this had ever happened and the Roman Catholic hierarchy anxiously questioned him as to what God looked like. Despite their attempts, the priest refused to answer. Eventually they took him to Rome where the Pope demanded to know what God looked like. He finally replied, "She was Chinese"!

Think about it!

Once you have got the answers from your own questioning, have the courage and maturity to seek OTHER PEOPLE'S OPINIONS – your wife's, your superiors', your co-workers' and ask someone from outside your own business environment. These opinions can be very valuable because you may be missing something, which is perfectly obvious to an outsider, and other people often perceive things so very differently. Such opinions can sometimes rape your own ideas and avoid your management suicide.

There áre three angles to the question of self-concept:

What we are? What we think we are?, What other people think we are?.

Be prepared to criticise your own work regularly and be on the look out for telltale symptoms of your personal ineffectiveness and ineffectual habits and actions. Be ruthless in applying the 20/80 rule because:

20% OF WHAT YOU DO INFLUENCES 80% OF YOUR SUCCESS.

FEEDBACK
How family, peers & associates see self

SELF CONCEPT

DEFENSES

WHAT SELF SEEMS TO BE: IMAGE

How self sees itself.
Past. Present. Future.

QUOTE

"Ah wad some power the giftie to gae us, tae see ourselves as other see us. Frae many a mistake would it frae us and foolish notion."

Robbie Burns

Asking questions – The socratic method

"I have six honest serving men,
They taught me all a knew,
Their names are What and Why and When,
Where and How and Who."

Rudyard Kipling.

My Granny used to say that asking questions
was the launching pad to all wisdom!

This logical, critical and analytical approach
can be used to solve many different problems:
innovation, systems design, cost reduction
and, especially, self-improvement.

Ask these questions about your work:

What am I really doing?	-	Result, priorities, key effectiveness areas.
How am I doing it?	-	Self work-study, productivity.
Why do I do certain things?	-	Work elimination
When do I do it?	-	Time, re-scheduling
Who else could do it?	-	Delegation.
Where do I do it?	-	Location, duplication.

The greatest cause of managerial ineffectiveness is - overwork

"NO! - I can't be bothered to see any crazy salesman - we've got a battle to fight!"
Are you so embroiled in your daily battles that you do not stop to think?

Portrait of an ineffective executive

They generally have a false idea as to how they spend their time and they get little mileage from their working hours. They are a TIME BUM.

They are confused about their priorities. There is little evidence of THINKING, preparation and planning.
They suffer from bad personal organisation. They allow themselves to be frequently interrupted – never scheduling long periods to execute their management functions.

They confuse ACTIVITY WITH ACTION.

They judge themselves on the basis of WORK INPUTS rather than WORK OUTPUTS.

They are blind to the important, have a facility to miss the point and a passion for detail.

Their self-discipline is extremely weak And they let personal preferences dictate Their actions.

They are involved with far too much paperwork. Their desk is piled high with paper to give the impression of working like a Trojan Horse! They are a phoney pony!

They talk too much and the telephone is their greatest downfall and enemy.

They 'grasshop', jumping from one Uncompleted job to another, involving criminal duplication of time and energy.

They are anxious and indecisive, they side step final decisions.
They have poor and undeveloped subordinates – pays peanuts and gets monkeys – and is indifferent to the well being of their staff.
Their days are too fragmented; they make ineffective decisions and do not get much job satisfaction.
They suffer from inertia, stick to tradition and are a managerial pigmy.
Their delegation is poor – they are a one-man band,
Their physical and emotional health is poor.
They are given to distraction, impatience, indolence and procrastination.
Their communications are abysmal.
Their leadership qualities are like a human chamber of horrors.
They use the politics of the ivory tower, the psychology of the nursery and the economics of the madhouse.

Portrait of an ineffective leader
or the human chamber of horrors

They are head hunted by companies wishing to make tax losses.

They run their team like a priest in a brothel.

They cannot do big things therefore they do little things in a big way.

They are the boss rather than the leader and their most important word in "I".

They give little direction to their team and they are completely "in the dark" about the business, its objectives and news.

They exploit fear rather than encouragement.

They offer no incentive to people and never challenge or stretches them.

They are unfriendly and not prepared to listen to personal as well as job problems. They are indecisive and cannot make decisions.

They look for weaknesses in people and situations rather than strengths.

They blame people when things go wrong rather than finding out the cause of failure. They create boredom and fatigue out of work rather than making it a game, a challenge and fun.

They are far too emotional, are introvert and make decisions on emotion rather than logic.

Their mind organisation is like an unmade bed.

They are secretive and play office politics. They are unable to get the best out of people or awaken talent.

They have no ability to enthuse and create a congenial atmosphere where productivity, performance and job enrichment will be enhanced.

Their staff consider them cowardly, tight faced, arrogant, egotistical, unreliable, bloody-minded, untrustworthy, lazy, reactionary, intellectually vulgar, depressing, catastrophic, hopelessly narrow minded, brash, disastrously stupid, devious, completely ineffective and an ape.

Checklist - Self Rating Assessment

Circle the appropriate number following
each effective executive practice.

1 is poor: 2 is mediocre: 3 is average:
4 is very good or considerably
above average: 5 is excellent.

Be honest; let other people rate you
also. Total your score below.

1. Achieving Results	1	2	3	4	5	19. Planning	1	2	3	4	5
2. Analytical Powers	1	2	3	4	5	20. Positive Thinking	1	2	3	4	5
3. Communication Ability	1	2	3	4	5	21. Personal Productivity	1	2	3	4	5
4. Concentration	1	2	3	4	5	22. Public Speaking	1	2	3	4	5
5. Control	1	2	3	4	5	23. Salesmanship	1	2	3	4	5
6. Current Performance	1	2	3	4	5	24. Self- Discipline	1	2	3	4	5
7. Decision Making Ability	1	2	3	4	5	25. Self-Organisation	1	2	3	4	5
8. Delegation Skills	1	2	3	4	5	26. Stick ability	1	2	3	4	5
9. Developing Others	1	2	3	4	5	27. Stress Tolerance	1	2	3	4	5
10. Happiness	1	2	3	4	5	28. Success	1	2	3	4	5
11. Health	1	2	3	4	5	29. Time Management	1	2	3	4	5
12. Interruptions	1	2	3	4	5	30. Worry	1	2	3	4	5
13. Knowing priorities Key effectiveness areas	1	2	3	4	5						
14. Leadership skills	1	2	3	4	5						
15. Listening	1	2	3	4	5						
16. Luck	1	2	3	4	5						
17. Money Management	1	2	3	4	5						
18. Organisation Skills	1	2	3	4	5						

Highest Standards

There is only one kind of acceptable performance – that which measures to the highest standards. The highest standard for each individual is that which his conscience tells him is best. The standards the individual's conscience sets are determined by his environment, associations, knowledge, training and any personal self-improvement programmes. Demand from yourself the very best and expect it from others.

Continuing individual exposure to the impact of highly motivated people and institutions raises standards and life becomes more and more of a challenge to attain higher and higher ideals. This is growth: this is life.

The attainment of standards requires motivation, courage, practice and self-discipline. Inactivity, protection from exposure and constant avoidance of challenges will prevent attainment of acceptable standards and will not allow the individual to grow. Challenge yourself frequently, think big, every challenge won leads to greater confidence and success, Give some thought to what your own standards are and how well you are lining up to them. No one is perfect – there is always someone better or worse than you. Constant endeavour means progress. Believe that anything less than attainment of these standards is unsatisfactory.

To some this is a challenge, while to others it is an alibi.

My granny was plump and cuddly, old and wise, was married to a Mexican and had only one tooth – we used to call her Juanita!!

She used to say that around so many things in life is a lot of wooliness; if we are to pierce successfully our own wooliness, we have got to ask questions!

The Lazy Man's Approach

My grandfather was an old American Indian fighter – my Granny was the old Indian. The old guy had a great sense of humour, deep wisdom and always seemed to achieve much although never appearing to do a lot. He taught me in retrospect the attributes of a lazy man's approach to work, life and accomplishment. I have since learned to look out and identify people accused of laziness because on so many occasions they were not lazy but in fact effective. Lazy people somehow inherently think of the quickest and easiest ways of doing things. They have arrived at methods which are effective and they are clear thinkers. They use their personal resources to the full and always get their priorities right.

That we can learn from them such an offbeat philosophy has long been in my mind and then I heard of a chairman of an International Pharmaceutical Manufacturer responsible for picking the top international executives. His company had done a great deal for Society and at the same time made a superlative profit return on the capital employed. On being asked what was the top attribute he looked for when picking his executives he answered that his preferred quality and what he looked for and praised was one of well-controlled laziness.

"The intelligent are lazy" as the Germans say. Lazy people have a sense of priority because they do not want to do anything unnecessary. Lazy people write short letters for the same reason.

They delegate because they would rather sit back and let others get on with anything that is not essential for them to do themselves. They spurn unnecessary and idiotic detail, which ensures that they do not interfere without cause in the minutiae of what their staffs are doing. They are inventive in pursuit of more efficient ways of acquiring time in which to be idle – the wheel was no doubt thought up by such a fellow, disgusted with the labour of pulling a sledge.

Best of all, such, executives last longer. A conscientiously lazy man could probably cat-nap spiritually if not physically, gets relaxingly high from time to time at lunchtime, turns up late for the office without half killing himself with guilt, and plans round the world trips with the essential 'swanning days' – out to the Taj Mahal or to Melbourne racecourse – that will help him avoid burning himself out prematurely.

Effectiveness means getting results

Have you considered what effectiveness really is?

Very simply, it is the ability to give attention to the right things and concentrate on the truly important activities in your work. It is achieving results and making things happen.

It is exceedingly hard to convince and get across even to the most intelligent people that a manager or executive doing something very industriously and diligently BUT – DOING THE WRONG KIND OF THING is a most meaningless and criminally wasteful uneconomic exercise.

Many people say they are working efficiently, but efficiency is concerned with doing things rightly, overlooking the fact that one is spending time and energy doing rightly and well things that ought not to have been done in the first place.

Examples come to mind of Managing Directors not doing sufficient "thinking" or "managing", designers working on the wrong kind of machines, salesmen selling unprofitable products or managers with false priorities and doing work which could and should be delegated.

Far too many people seem to be concerned with effort. It is the basis on which many are paid and is certainly the criteria by which they assess their seeming efficiency. They go home at the days end and the conclusions are that the greater the degree of tiredness the greater has been their effort and the better they have done the job. How terribly sad!

Rubbish can never justify the effort to produce it – the more effective measure is of course RESULTS – getting things done. Results (more profit, ideas, innovation, new customers, achievements, productivity increases) really count in the final analysis and we must always judge ourselves and other people on the basis of these.

DO NOT CONFUSE ACTIVITY WITH ACCOMPLISHMENT and fall into the activity trap.

Never substitute activity for achievement. Look out for the workaholic in you and signs of inflexibility and short sightedness because you are beavering around but accomplishing little.

Give much thought to your KEY EFFECTIVENESS AREAS – (on the following page) and concentrate your energies on the part of the job on which you will be truly judged.

A manager had two important things on his desk – his feet!!

Your philosophy must be to – WORK SMARTER RATHER THEN HARDER.

Your key effectiveness areas

List the main priorities in your work:

Other peoples' opinions of what your priorities should be:

List the main priorities in your life:

P.S. This space is insufficient. When you do this for yourself use a whole sheet for each section.

13

Key effectiveness areas

In any discussion of priorities and self-organisation knowing your key effectiveness areas is critical.

You will achieve little unless you CLEARLY know:

The key results you must achieve.

The performance standards and criteria by which you will be judged.

The control information you require to monitor your progress.

Managerial effectiveness is the extent to which a manager achieves the output requirements of his job. We must carefully and creatively THINK about key result areas, involve others in their determination and not be afraid to emulate successful people and companies. Alert and aware managers seek out and research the factors in others' success.

Your own effectiveness areas can be written on page 13.
For guidance, here are a few. Remember that you should concentrate on OUTPUTS not INPUTS.

Profit, Cash Flow and Money – the right financial strategy (including using O.P.M. – Other people's money).

Productivity and an adequate return on investment – at least 30%.

Nurturing effective people, management succession, measuring and getting productivity, team spirit, giving job fulfilment and having good labour relations.

Concentrate on the right market, new customers, product profitability, the right prices, the market share and service.

Research and development, innovation and use of the new technology.

Control Costs.

Maximum productivity of assets and minimisation of stock levels.

Effective administration, management information systems and paperwork simplification.

Your key resources are not being used in low profit areas.

Tax strategy and legitimate minimisation of payments.

Quality programmes.

Practicing management.

All these result areas would be measurable and quantified rather than qualitative. They should be specific, action orientated rather than activity centred and should be realistic and attainable. Remember to build in "stretch" and set time targets.

As far as subordinates are concerned make sure

They know clearly what their job is, that it is worth doing and they have a good job description.

What is expected of them – their duties and targets, quantified and to a time scale if possible.

They want to know regularly – how they are performing – the good news and the bad.

Help and guidance from you.

They want to be rewarded for their effectiveness and contribution.

SPEND MORE TIME MAKING PROFITS
WHAT AM I HERE FOR?

15

Priorities

Think regularly of your fundamental objectives and direction. Keep your mind on the important
matters and remember the law of the IMPORTANT
FEW AND THE TRIVIAL MANY.

Try to think clearly in a peaceful environment and, to help you to be objective, ask for the opinions
of others – your family, your superiors, your staff
and, even, outsiders – because they can offer a fresh view.

Look ahead to the future and do not dwell on the
past. Use foresight and drive and manage by anticipation.

Use some of the principles of Company Corporate
Planning to prepare long range plans for the next
five years. Consider a strategic environment appraisal. Look at the political, economic, technological and sociological environment and see how they apply to you.

Focus on the opportunities around you and not the problems – THINK BIG.

Have the courage to choose your own direction rather than climbing on the bandwagon. Have confidence in yourself and use your imagination. Make sure you know what all your resources are and use and exploit them fully. Remember that the more you do in life, the more you are capable of doing.

Once you have decided on your priorities, keep a close watch on the situation and measure your performance regularly. Set aside at least 10% of your working week for this activity and the more you become involved with this approach to working, the more you will enjoy it. Remind yourself of your priorities weekly and avoid getting too involved with anything not in your plans unless it is a potential opportunity.

What a pity it is that we do not have a loud speaker blasting out our key objectives every day.

Remember: SET GOALS

MAKE PLANS

TAKE ACTION

Also remember to use the right amount of time on the truly important aspects of your work.

16

Planning

An aircraft pilot would be barred and criminally prosecuted if he took off without a flight plan. Few of us would think of starting off on a long journey by car without first obtaining a map on which we could plot our route.

Yet, business and life are infinitely more important journeys and are seldom plotted half so well as a three-day trip to another city. Many of us wander aimlessly, turning this way and that – backtracking, detouring and bumping over rough roads. Most managers will admit that they do not do enough planning.

Planning involves thinking. Thinking about where we want to go to, how we are going to get there and what resources are available to make it all possible.

Lord Thomson of Fleet, a most successful entrepreneur, was once asked if he had any advice which he could pass on to a young man who wished to be successful. He replied that, "If one wants to be successful, one must think, one must think, think, think until it hurts".

Planning means the use of foresight and forcing yourself to look ahead. It means determining objectives and targets. Without these all operations lack direction, you do not foresee problems, results lack meaning and the implication for future policies are dwarfed by the pressure of the present. We have heard so many times the regrets of people who wish they had looked ahead and acted accordingly.

By spending a lot of your time on planning and crystal ball gazing you are compelled to look ahead. You will be ready for change in conditions and circumstances and be able to make the best use of your time and resources.

Good management should be called 'management by anticipation'. All managers need a system that helps to anticipate and avoid tomorrow's troubles rather than re-hashing yesterday's problems. Unfortunately, many managers devote too much attention to fire fighting and past events when the right time for management action is BEFORE things go wrong, not after.

Working with Field Marshal Montgomery I became familiar with his saying that "he won more battles then the Germans – because he planned them better". Indeed he was a meticulous planner. Generals win battles through good planning and companies through corporate planning, produce a higher return on the capital employed. Through good planning managers are more effective, more successful and life runs smoothly.

The basic process of planning is:

Establish objectives or set goals to be achieved.

Determine where you or your organisation is in relation to that goal.

Know exactly your resources, your strengths and weaknesses.

Determine which factors in the environment will help you or your organisation reach its goal and which factors will act as barriers. Predict or forecast what factors will appear in the future and how the present factors will change.

Develop a plan or a set of actions and policies for reaching the goal. Generate a set of alternative courses of action, evaluate them and then act accordingly.

Plan for business achievements, for money, your career, self-improvement and your effective living. Use a telescope and not a microscope.

In your business make sure there are plans in every area of activity but particularly in finance, research, marketing and sales, organisation, production, people and purchasing.

Field Marshal Montgomery

A leader with a passion for planning.

QUOTE

"The ideal Chief Executive Officer would be a poet, a historian and a student of weather maps. Writing poetry will give him precision in thought and language, history will teach him strategy, while studying weather maps will teach him decision making under uncertainty."

Bill Redden

Checklist - Your planning and organisation

Are objectives achieved within stipulated time scales?

Do jobs come out on time and of the right standard?

Does the work run smoothly?

Is there evidence of your planning? Do all staff know about the advantages of planning?

Do you distribute work in the most effective way?

Do you set yourself the right priorities? Do you decide priorities correctly within your authority?

Do you delegate as far as possible?

Do you make the best use of other service departments?

Does your department cooperate effectively in the team as a whole?

Thinking back over recent wastage of manpower or non-achievement, could better planning have avoided it?

Do you make time for special creative work?

How many of your tasks are rush jobs?

Are you using all available resources and the best methods available?

Are you studying the use of your own time so that you are doing the things which are really effective?

Do you know the costs covering the operations under your control? Are they under constant scrutiny?

Has the improvement in the efforts and results for which you are responsible been good enough during the last twelve months? If not, what were the obstacles?

Are your current plans and targets providing a firm base for a strong future? Are they sufficiently geared to customer needs?

Can you more effectively utilise the knowledge and skills of your specialist and managerial colleagues and subordinates and are you supporting them with constructive comments and actions?

Are you taking full and immediate advantage of the education and training which you and your subordinates are undergoing?

Meetings and procedures are an integral part of the process of managing. Are you using them effectively to focus on objectives and results?

Do you ensure that all relevant information has been assembled and that the appropriate techniques have been used before making the decision?

Having weighed up the alternatives, do you make decisions without delay and communicate them clearly to your subordinates?

Are you and your subordinates properly in the picture and is it the right picture? Is your two-way communication really working?

You cannot conceive how much time you will save by it, nor how much better everything you do will be done. The mind of a man who has a business but no method nor order is an unordered mass which men call chaos. Prevail upon yourself only to observe good order and never to neglect it. Thereafter, you will find such convenience and advantage arising everywhere. I tell you with pleasure that order, method and more activity of mind are all that you want to make, some day or other, a considerable figure in business.

QUOTE

"Now that you are soon to be a man of business, I heartily wish you would immediately begin to be a man of method, nothing contributing more to facilitate and dispatch business than method and order. Have order and method in your accounts, in your reading, in the allotment of your time, in short in everything."

Lord Chesterfield
(Letters to his son 1754)

Organisation

"Order is heaven's first law" – Confucius.

Those who are able to direct themselves towards specific, clearly stated objectives are using effective work methods. Good personal organisation is an indication of maturity and well-organised thought whereas not having clear goals and efficient work habits suggests immaturity and disorder with the consequent results of wasted effort, uneconomic activity and chaos.

An immature manager starts many projects and finishes few; goes in many directions and finds that his efforts are dissipated. He does not display a systematic approach to his activities and it is like comparing a child to an adult. He constantly 'grass hops' and attempts to do too many things at the same time.

Only organisation can enable you to follow a straight line towards effectiveness and the accomplishment of your objectives. Without organisation, you will go around in vague purposeless circles, feeling frustrated and getting nowhere in spite of all your efforts and stress will be your constant companion.

Begin to organise by thinking out your priorities. See them clearly – in burning red letters across the sky. Stick to these priorities and avoid trivia.

All managers should learn and apply the point of the old nursery rhyme: -

Pussy cat, Pussy cat, where have you been?
I've been to London to look at the Queen,
Pussy cat, Pussy cat what did you see there?
I saw a little mouse under the chair.

Do you see the small things rather than the big things?
Organisation means making sure you see the big and the right things and concentrating on key effectiveness areas.

Knowing the things you want to do and doing them in the right order is the essence of organisation. Divide every job into a series of small steps, then tackle them one by one in the right order. Nurture methods of doing your work efficiently; get rhythm and discipline and rank things in order of importance. Disorganised people can usually see the whole job and are overwhelmed by its magnitude. Focus your mind on one step at a time and make haste slowly.

START with writing or reviewing your own and your peoples' JOB DESCRIPTIONS. This means thinking about and defining the work to be done by you and your people. Then establish the positions and the structure needed to do it, setting out accountability for the results to be achieved and creating effective teamwork among the various people involved in attaining these goals. Make sure there are clear lines of authority and communication as well as scope for delegation.

Good order is the foundation of all good things.

What makes a manager effective?

The doyen of American management philosophers, Peter Drucker, in his excellent book, "The Effective Executive", tells us that the only person in abundant supply is the universal incompetent!

Managers are concerned with knowledge work and their productivity is measured in their ability to get things done. This is effectiveness. Knowledge work is not defined by quantity but by results and these results reflect themselves in the business showing that the manager is doing a good job – i.e. really managing and putting into action all the principles of good management.

Industry, intelligence, imagination and knowledge are all wasted in any manager who has not acquired the ability to convert these into results. The greatest wisdom is meaningless without effective action and behaviour.

The measurement of effectiveness is, of course, the ability to get things done, to make things happen successfully and to achieve results. To measure success, achievements must always be compared with initial resources.

Very few companies really endeavour to measure actively the effectiveness of their top people and make them more accountable for their actions and decisions. There is not an overwhelming supply of truly competent managers who are constantly alert to their performance in the key effectiveness areas and who are willing to stand up and be counted. The practice of increasing the effectiveness of top managers is an area of neglect and deserves greater priority as a way of improving achievement and performance. A good manager may not be particularly logical, but if they are perceptive in what they are doing, the area of increased effectiveness may well be his best chance of raising the level of their achievements and job satisfaction.

Yet many managers have not even stopped to consider what effectiveness really is, what it consists of and how it can be learned. True effectiveness comes in a mix of managers from those who are highly educated to those with no formal academic qualifications. Effective managers use logic, perception and intuition and they think that effectiveness, as Peter Drucker tells us, is no more than a complex of practices. Practices can always be learnt and mastered if we have common sense, a strong will, lots of self-discipline and 'stickability'. Practices are, in fact, deceptively simple and even young children have no difficulty with them.

Ten effective practices

positive thinking
communications
priorities
time
strengths
motivation
self organisation
contribution
results

Ten effective practices

If we are to make practices automatic so that they become unthinking, a conditioned reflex and a firmly established habit, there are TEN salient points to follow, which should make up our overall philosophy:

1) The practice of daily THINKING. Force yourself to do a little thinking each day.

2) The practice of good self-organisation and making all routine matters habit.

3) The practice of knowing where your time goes and working systematically at time management and getting mileage out of your working day.

4) The practice of gearing your efforts to results rather than work. Judge yourself on the basis of outputs not inputs. Start out with a question – what results are expected of me – rather than questioning the amount of work to be done.

5) The practice of identifying and building on strengths – your own, other people's, those of superiors, colleagues and subordinates. Do not build on weaknesses: do not start out with the things you cannot do.

6) The practice of concentrating on the few major areas where superior performance will produce outstanding results. Force yourself to set priorities and stay with priority decisions. First things first, second things not at all.

Otherwise, you get nothing worthwhile done.

7) The practise of making good decisions: judgements based on thoughtful decision making techniques.

8) The practice of 'handling' people and obtaining productivity and co-operation from them.

9) The practice of being good at communications and passing on understanding.

10) The practice of positive mental attitude.

If one cannot increase the supply of a resource, one must increase its yield and effectiveness by the use of these practices is the only tool to make the resources of ability and knowledge yield more and better results.

How to have will power

Being effective is simply a question of rigid self-discipline. It means having strong will power and forcing yourself to do the right things and avoid waste and inefficiency. Habit is a group of practices. It is not easy to cultivate good habits, but, once formed, they are a dividend for life.

The question of habit formation is nowhere more important than in the case of training the will. Habit is simply repeating automatically, mental and physical acts and needs only constant practice. If we are always finding ourselves doing something we ought not to do or not doing something we should do, the cause is weak will.

An average batsman can make himself into a county player by just practising. It is no coincidence that the more you practice the luckier you become. The batsman plods away until he has formed the habit of playing with a straight bat, of playing his strokes correctly and making eye and wrist movements come together in perfect unison. Nothing else but a series of repeated acts has been responsible – plus the determination to succeed.

Tackle the problem of will power on similar lines. If you desire strong muscles, exercise. If you desire a strong will, exercise that too. It is not enough to have a half-hearted idea of strengthening your will, it takes positive action.

Think the matter out in detail. Weigh up your problem. Start the process with a clear vision of what needs to be done and a strong determination to see the thing through. Be as serious about it on Thursday as you were on Monday. Unremitting effort is essential for success. Tell yourself that you are improving daily; such self-congratulation can be a powerful aid to your success.

To nurture your self-discipline, each day try to do something which you do not like doing.

QUOTE

"If I had six hours to cut down a tree, I would spend three of them sharpening the axe."

Abraham Lincoln

Habit

The greatest force governing the human body is HABIT. From getting up in the morning to lying down at night 90% of our actions are automatic. Few people, however, turn actions into habits with the result that they spend a good part of the day deciding or regretting things that they ought hardly to be conscience of at all. Consequently, mental energy, effort and time are used up on trivial matters when there are more important considerations.

An ineffective manager is someone with an indecisive mind who simply has not taken the trouble to form enough habits to set their mind free for higher work. They are generally miserable and allow their nervous system to be their enemy rather than their ally.

Concentration is an example of a good habit. The ability to concentrate is the characteristic of all creative and productive minds and it is nothing more than the ability to ignore diversions, however enticing.

Industry, stamina, clear thinking and self-discipline are all a question of habit formation. There is no getting away from it, you have to make yourself work and be your own taskmaster. With such an approach the acquisition of the right habits can double your daily output.

Make thinking a habit with daily practice and sooner or later you will realise the rewards. Think in an active sense using the brain as a dynamo to manufacture originality and thought FORCE.

SELF-DISCIPLINE

When it comes to promoting greater personal effectiveness, self-discipline is the name of the game. Many of the ideas in this book are not new; they are simply matters of common sense, which deep down you know you should have been applying to your work and life.

A story, which well illustrates self-discipline, is that of a farmer's boy who was 'messing' around with the farmer's wife when the farmer caught him. He dragged him into a barn and put a certain part of his anatomy into a vice. The vice was turned and locked and the farmer's boy was in excruciating pain. The farmer left him only to return in a few minutes with a Black and Decker electric saw. "You're not going to do that, are you?" said the boy. "No", replied the farmer, "you are – I'm going to set the barn on fire!"

This illustrates quite clearly that sometimes we do not like doing things – but it is usually in our best interests!

Self-discipline and strong will power are the foundations of personal achievement.

Recognising strengths and weaknesses

Stick to the things you are good at that is the message that rings loud and clear.

The ability to recognise strengths, your own and those of your subordinates and superiors, and knowing how to exploit them is a vitally important ingredient of success. Endeavour to nurture and expand your strengths and concentrate on them to the utmost.

Get to know them and also your weaknesses by carefully completing the following page, you need to be aware of weaknesses (being a poor public speaker, giving in to interruptions and lacking in self discipline) because recognition of these is the first steps to remedying them.

Note also that your own awareness of your strengths and weaknesses is insufficient. Many a millionaire is rich because he used other people's money. In the same way, you can profit by using other people's opinions.

How we see ourselves is often different to the view other's have. Therefore, a valuable part of the exercise is to seek their opinions and comments. Ask two people from your business environment and someone from your family to complete the page following. The results can be quite surprising. Do not be too alarmed if weaknesses seem to be highlighted because a person who does not have a weakness does not have a strength.

See the following sentence as clearly as you would a stag's head against the sunset:

EXPLOIT YOUR STRENGTHS AND DO WHAT YOU ARE GOOD AT!

And as for your weaknesses – remedy them or give other people the work you are not so good at!

Apply the same approach with staff. Use horses for courses and exploit their strengths. Regularly review each member of staff, finding their weaknesses and deciding on the appropriate action. Keep this information on record cards. Tackle these weaknesses courageously and, where they are motivational and not associated with skills or knowledge, handle the problem in an objective way by frank talks. This can be psychologically difficult to instigate and carry out in a fair, straightforward and unembarrassed way. Nevertheless, anybody who accepts the role of manager must take on the responsibility of this task.

After locating and identifying weaknesses in people, specify the areas of improvement and regularly review progress.

The discipline of actually writing down strengths and weaknesses is worthwhile and can provide a background for general discussion about work performance between management and staff.

Analyse your strengths and weaknesses

My strengths	Other peoples' opinions of my strengths

My weaknesses	Other peoples' opinions of my weaknesses

Self perception

Organised thought, meditation and careful development of self-perception are the long used tools of those who seek greater life fulfilment. No matter how successful you are now or no matter how well adjusted life may seem, there is a need on everyone's part to develop an analytical self evaluation and appraisal so as to have greater control over the affairs of your life.

In your map of life consider the under mentioned.

Where are you today in your life span?

Birth _____Death

Write down a few answers to what you are: i.e. parent, accountant, manager, entrepreneur, moneymaker, philosopher, Christian, humanist etc.

Place them in order.

Write down the key points in your own obituary.

QUOTE

"It is simple. Work hard, use the best technology, produce unique goods at low costs, develop markets, take responsibility at the top for all important decisions, commit all resources to achieving targets, think big."

Akio Morita, Chairman, Sony Corporation

"The Thinker"

Life Inventory

Write down the key milestones in your life both in your personal and work life.

_____

_____

_____

_____

_____

_____

_____

_____

What short-term tactical plans do you have to achieve in this next year.

_____

_____

_____

_____

_____

_____

_____

What are your future strategic goals and plans?

_____

_____

_____

_____

_____

_____

_____

_____

TH!NK
What do you really want from life

TAKE STOCK OF YOUR POSSIBILITIES

30

Decision making

Decision-making is one of the tasks of the manager. It is a specific executive task, which deserves concentration and special treatment. They are expected by virtue of position or knowledge to make decisions that have significant impact on the entire organisation, its performance and results.

Effective Managers therefore make effective decisions. They concentrate on the important ones, not on many decisions and think through strategy

Basically decision-making is thinking and the person who can think is always the master of the person who can only do. Even better the people who rise highest in the world are those who can both think and do. Thinking is an ability involving examining the matter, identifying the specific problems, fragmenting the problem into manageable parts, suggesting possible solutions, testing those solutions and evaluating the results.

If the manager is mature, they are objective, get the facts, evaluate the situation on its merits, disassociates themselves form personal feelings or bias, which might prejudice their decisions. They use judgement, separates the significant from the insignificant and fact from value in the decision making process. Judgements are made on the experience they have already had.

Fact is fact – opinion is opinion. Exercise great care in the search of truth, which is very often a matter of perspective. Looking at the same objective or situation different human beings see it in radically different ways.

We must learn to understand and ultimately to value the different perspectives and models of reality.

Make sure you first identify the problem – very often it is solved in the process of identifying it. Make sure you are clear in your mind what it is and write it down. It may make sense to ask the question how you arrived at the actual problem, translate it and interpret. Endeavour to recognise unstated assumptions and bring fact together, to form a new whole – synergy. Refer to history and that in life so much is repetition.

Once clearly identifying it get all the relevant facts and make sure that they are presented to you in a form that you understand simply, clearly and promptly.

Consult and seek other people's opinions - OPO's – and also dissenting opinion because other views can stimulate your thinking and a mix of ideas can blend into a good decisive plan.

List the alternative course of action available and then write down the disadvantages and advantages for each alternative. Think in money terms and quantify on a cost benefit analysis basis. Use capital investment appraisal techniques, or operational research techniques if the matter is of great substance. Consider the affects and ramifications of your courses of action.

Remember that decision-making is not a popularity contest and the question should be WHAT is right, rather than WHO is right? Sometimes these decisions take COURAGE and one should remember that in the rat race only the rat's win.

A decision is a judgment in the final analysis and it is made by people and therefore not perfect. Many people put off making a decision because they are seeking perfection.
Perfection means paralysis and immobility – that is not a human attribute. Recognise this and make the decision. When you cannot get all you own way know about COMPROMISE, which could very well be a solution rather than the frustration of stalemate. If courses of action have equal advantages, spin a coin but at least MAKE A DECISION.

Once the decision has been made make sure that you communicate it and let all parties concerned know about it. "Nobody ever told me" is so often heard in industry.

Sometimes when you have great difficulty in coming to a decision try using your SUBCONSCIOUS MIND, which can be more effective than you conscious mind. Without making a decision consider the problem comprehensively and forget about it for a while. The mind will let it simmer and steaming subconscious thought and very soon the appropriate decision will be arrived at. Sometimes it pays to sleep on important decisions.

Not all decisions are important ones, and we must learn to identify those, which we should make immediately or within 24 hours. Do not put these off – DO IT NOW and take these decisions when the problem presents itself otherwise there is a duplication of effort and further problems will mount up leading to tension, greater stress and a worsening situation.

Decision making around here is like two elephants mating, says a friend of mine. It is done at a very high level with lots of shrieking and howling and it takes two years for anything to happen!

Insure that you give time to important decisions and do not make snap judgements.

Can we learn from history

In Machiavelli's book, "The Prince", he attempts to analyse current and relevant management problems in the light of experience and observations from history. It is a pity that Machiavelli's name is synonymous with sinister and unscrupulous intrigue as his main purpose was simply to analyse what practices had brought political success in the past and to deduce from them what principles ought to be followed for the success of the present.

There are always historic parallels in one's self-assessment, in life and, particularly, in decision making and we can always learn from them. Hannibal won his battles by starting them early in the day; Richard I fought other people's battles and neglected his own country; Elizabeth I was too autocratic; George III listened to 'Yes' men and lost us America; Napoleon overstretched himself with inadequate resources; Nelson had a blind eye to authority; Hitler repeated Napoleon's mistake of overstretching himself; and President Regan operates with more style, perhaps, than substance.

Vice Admiral Horatio Nelson

Life runs in cycles – joy then sadness, peaks and troughs, booms and depressions. Perhaps, as well as studying and analysing history, we can analyse our own and other peoples' tracks records and learn from them.

In this way the study of the past can allow the young to have the wisdom of the old.

Analysing success

Many managers spend the vast bulk of their time and effort in analysing and curing failure. What they need to do is to analyse success. When you concentrate on failure, at best, you know what not to do, at worst, you become mesmerised by it and blunder into the same trap again. Wallowing in failure and handing out blame all too often seems to be the order of the day.

If you concentrate on success, however small, and see why it happened then apart from the psychological effects (which every great general has understood) you can consciously plan to reproduce the success and expand it. Concentrate on the analysis of success, run with success, it is our strengths we have to exploit. Learn from failure.

Extensive studies by behavioural scientists reveal:

Success generally leads to a raising of the level of aspiration, failure to a lowering. Similarly, the stronger the success the greater is the probability of a greater attainment.

Shifts in levels of aspiration are in part a function of changes in the subject's confidence and his ability to attain goals.

Failure is more likely than success to lead to withdrawal in the form of avoiding setting a level of aspiration. The effects of failure on levels of aspiration are more varied than those of success.

Conversely, people who experience failure tend to lose interest in their work; lower their standards of achievement; lose confidence in themselves, give up quickly; fear any new tasks and refuse to try new methods or accept new jobs; expect failure; escape from failure by day-dreaming; increase their difficulty in working with others; develop a tendency to blame others, to be over critical of the work of others and to get into trouble with other employees. It is worth remembering that when you speak of failure, you attract failure – when you speak of success, you attract success.

In search of excellence

In their book, "In Search of Excellence", Peters and Waterman, top American management consultants, studied 21 US companies noted for their excellence and researched the policies, philosophies and principles underlying success, profitability, survival and excellence. These companies (Boelng, IBM, McDonalds Hamburgers and others) got phenomenal mileage from the enthusiasm they generated amongst their employees about their products and customers. No company succeeds without proper leadership and without paying close attention to customers and profitability. All companies were action orientated, encouraged autonomy and entrepreneurship by pushing responsibility down, had lean administrations and, at the same time, tight/ lose controls. Their productivity through people was such that they inculcated the values and the excellent companies had a constant commitment to innovation, customer relations and leadership.

Outstanding amongst the philosophies was that of "management by wandering about" which is so neglected in many management functions – wandering about and meeting customers, staff, suppliers is the technology of the obvious.

Being brilliant at basics is a common sense approach, which very much reflects itself in success and profitability.

The whole thing is summed up in these words:

"The essence of Excellence is the thousand concrete, minute-to-minute actions performed by everyone in organisation to keep a company on its course. Excellent companies are brilliant on just a few basics: behaving with courtesy towards customers, providing a continuous array of innovative products and services, and above all, gaining the commitment, ingenuity and energy of all employees."

The simplest mnemonic which embodies the message of success is:
M.E.E. A. F.A.S.T. B.I.T.

These winning companies were concerned with Making money – they were profit orientated not product orientated, money came first; they Evaluated strengths and weaknesses – concentrating on the strengths; they Economised all of the time.

They constantly Asked questions about all spheres of their activities.

They Flattened company responsibility to all staff; they Admitted their failures – getting out of loss making situations quickly; they Shared the benefits of success with staff – praise, status money and equity interest; they Tightened up consistently.

They Behaved unto others as they would expect others to behave unto them – customer and staff orientated; they Improved efficiency all of the time; they Thought simply, directly and clearly at all times.

"WORK SHOULD BE MORE FUN THAN FUN"

Management by exception

Management by exception requires that an executive develops policies and plans for the organisational unit for which they are responsible; delegates full authority to subordinates to act in accordance with approval policies and plans; expects deviations from approved policies to be brought to them and then appraises them in terms of the approved policies and plans. Under these circumstances, the executive need not concern themselves with the details of daily operations – they only deal with 'exceptions' to approved policies and plans.

Thus an executive who practices management by exception can devote substantially more of their time to planning the future; developing the organisation structure; selecting personnel; co-ordinating the activities of the various elements that make up their organisation; considering and deciding on major deviations from established objectives, policies, programmes or procedures; and reviewing the overall results of operations. Unless a major deviation is brought to their attention, they can safely assume that the business or unit is being managed in accordance with approved policies and plans.

To practise management by exception most effectively an executive needs three things: (1) ability to delegate; (2) confidence in the ability of their subordinates to apply sound judgement and to make sound independent decisions on problems that come within the scope of responsibilities and authorities delegated to their respective positions: and (3) a well designed and up-to-date system of 'Management Information'.

The concept of management by exception is one of the most valuable and important in the science of modern management. Without it, an executive managing even a relatively small and simple operation can become hopelessly bogged down in routine decisions, meetings and paperwork. On the other hand, full application of this concept makes it possible for a skilled executive to manage an extensive and complex organisation effectively without assuming an intolerable workload.

Delegation

Moses, who led his people out of the land of Egypt so successfully, completely failed and lost effectiveness when he became so impressed with his own knowledge and authority that he insisted on ruling personally on everything.

We cannot put a price on delegation, but without it we pay dearly. So many managers are loathe to delegate because they are insecure, they lack ability or their bad organisation through inflexibility and bad planning does not allow them to look ahead in order to work things out. If we are to become good managers – ones who can make better use of other men than they can make of themselves – we must DELEGATE.

Delegation means assigning the authority and responsibility for carrying out specific duties to a subordinate but still retaining accountability and being answerable for the results. If we do this regularly, nurturing and developing our delegation powers, we find that we have more time for our priorities – the parts of the job, which can make a significant contribution to our work and our organisation. Objectives are achieved, things are done quicker without reference to higher authority, delays are avoided and confidence is increased combined with better team spirit.

Aim to delegate at least 50% of your current work. By doing so, you are able to exploit not only the strengths of your people but, more particularly, your own strengths by retaining only the tasks you are actually being paid to do. A great many managers involve themselves in trivia and mental tasks for which they should be ashamed.

By delegating, you will develop and 'stretch' your people which will increase their self-confidence and reliance, get better value from them, train understudies and give them a more worthwhile job to do. Delegate decision-making. In the long-term, this is a good investment. Expect that occasionally mistakes will occur and be prepared for this. Make sure the individuals you delegate to have the necessary authority to carry out the tasks effectively and make sure that clear lines of authority and responsibility are established and recognised.

When you give out tasks, ensure whoever is doing it know: -

What you want, why you want it and why they should do it.

How best to do it.

When you want it.

When people do a job incorrectly, tell them frankly and cordially and when they do it well, praise them.

Delegation means establishing goals, giving responsibility and authority and motivating your people.

As in everything you do establish CONTROL systems, feedback, reports and control mechanisms that confirm the job is being done correctly.

Check up and try working on the exception principle. Go and see occasionally.

On correspondence you are passing on, code instructions:

Code 1. Take action – forget me
Code 2. Take action – advise result
Code 3. Look into the problem – suggest alternative course of action and then advise me.
Code 4. We will solve this one jointly.

BARRIERS TO DELEGATION

Good delegation can only be achieved through good communications and understanding with your people. The barriers are often because of an inflated self-worth assessment of the executive or because they are old fashioned or comes up with the term "it's quicker to do it myself". If you are working 60 hours a week maybe you can reduce this down to 30 hours with proper delegation.

Do not feel guilty about passing your work on, very often you have too much to do anyhow while your subordinates are not properly stretched. The big jobs in your work are thought and initiative. Swallow your pride and force yourself and be a good general.

Examine your work with the object of finding out whether the tasks you normally undertake could be carried out just as well, if not better, by a member of your staff. It is an undeniable fact that the executive so often takes on duties and responsibilities that could and should be delegated.

Examine all your tasks and ask the following questions:

Can the distribution of work between you and your fellow workers be improved?
Can you delegate more work to others and build up a more efficient team?
How can you delegate to leave yourself more free time to deal with the important things you should achieve?
Am I building a successful team?
Are the team members working together constructively?
Is each member of the team really pulling his or her weight?
Could one member achieve better results if they were to be put on another job? 'Horses for courses'
Is there a younger person within the company who could generate new impulses within the team?
Are you developing and training people, getting the best from them and judging them on their strengths?

Checklist on delegation

Good leaders get people "to do things they do not like – and like it!"

Here is a checklist to see how effective you are at getting your subordinates to make things happen. Look closely at each area in which you must answer "no" or a half hearted "yes".

Do I sell people on doing things?

Do I know what makes each subordinate tick?

Am I a good listener to employees?

Do I criticize in private?

Do I praise in public?

Do I offer constructive criticism?

Do I give credit where it is due?

Do I show personal interest in those working for me?

Do I give reasons when I ask that something be done?

Do I let my people know what is going on?

Am I consistent in disciplining when it is needed?

Do I show people that I have confidence in them?

Do I ask my subordinates for their ideas?

Do I give people a chance to help set goals or help make decisions?

Do my subordinates know where they stand at all times?

Do I give my instructions clearly so they are understood?

Do I look for solutions to the grievances of my subordinates?

Do I seek to develop those showing promise?

QUOTE

"I like work. It fascinates me. I fancy it and look at it for hours. I love to keep it by me. The idea of getting rid of it nearly breaks my heart."

Jerome K. Jerome

Tasks I could & should delegate

_____
_____
_____
_____
_____
_____
_____
_____
_____

To whom

_____
_____
_____
_____
_____
_____
_____
_____
_____

Action

_____
_____
_____
_____
_____
_____
_____
_____
_____

Time management

Of all the things that stand out in the practice of Effective Management the most important and paramount is that of **TIME MANAGEMENT**. If you would love life then do not squander time and in getting anything significant done undoubtedly it is how effectively time is used that reflects itself in our success.

Time is our scarcest resource and we can never get any more of it. Some mistakes can be corrected but not the mistake of wasted time and when time goes it is gone forever. It is the one thing that is rationed to everyone, and there is no black market at any price. It is a unique resource, its supply is inelastic, and it is perishable and cannot be stored. Yesterday's time is gone forever and cannot be replaced.

No man is paid for his time but he is paid for what use he makes of it and only used time in this respect is of value and use of ones time determines the space one occupies in this world. All successful people live each day as if it were their last and develop a keen respect for time.

Accordingly the analysis of ones time is the one easily demonstrated and systematic way to analyse ones work and to think through what really matters. Unless your time is managed nothing else can be and you will find time for all of your needs if you have properly organised it.

What can you really do about it, especially as you probably think that you know where your time goes and you are of the wishbone personality and intend to get it organised. Good intentions are seldom turned into achievement however and one must perpetually and constantly remind oneself of this key executive practice.

THE THREE STAGES IN EFFECTIVE TIME MANAGEMENT are as follows:

RECORD YOUR TIME
By keeping a time log and carrying out an in depth penetrating analysis of how your time is spent and used.

ORGANISE IT
Think about how to rearrange your work to get optimum self-utilization.

COMMAND AND CONTROL IT
Be in charge by perpetually being aware and in control of its use.

Time management means self-respect; by managing your time you are establishing your superior right to be at the top.

Time log

The purpose of maintaining and analysing a log is to give you an indication of how you spend your time and to enable you to organise your future personal performance by:

Eliminating work ensuring you are working on the right things, which will produce results and greater effectiveness.

Delegating more considering both current tasks and people available to accept them.

Showing possibilities for improvement and simplification of working methods and habits.

Improving your planning and personal organisation.

DAILY WORK & TIME LOG STUDY

Complete and study carefully the daily work log as illustrated. It is very necessary to obtain a general picture of your work structure which in all probability is different to the way you think you spend your time.

This simple form is all that is needed for the study and the tasks are coded to facilitate completion. Make sure you classify the activities correctly and that you record all interruptions. Record all tasks taking at least five minutes and for reliable results complete and study the log for at least two weeks and preferably one month. In many cases it might be well to continue it over a longer period,

making the study during say one week of each month or three days a week. It is obviously important for the time to be selected so that no special annual activity distorts the picture. You may also wish to continue the study to cover tasks performed outside normal working hours – watching television for example.

TIME LOG STUDY

When you have completed your time analysis to –

ELIMINATE NON PRODUCTIVE TIME WASTING ACTIVITIES

ASK THREE KEY QUESTIONS

WHAT AM I DOING THAT NEED NOT BE DONE AT ALL BY ME OR ANYONE ELSE? WHAT WOULD HAPPEN IF THIS WAS NOT DONE AT ALL?

WHICH OF MY ACTIVITIES SOMEONE ELSE COULD DO JUST AS WELL IF NOT BETTER?

AM I WASTING OTHER PEOPLE'S TIME?

IMPRINT the questions on your mind and continue to re-ask them regularly and review the answers.

ACTIVITY ANALYSIS SHEET

ACTIVITY CODING

1	Planning	5	Motivation	9	Telephone
2	Organization	6	Active Skill Time	10	Waiting
3	Coordination	7	Travelling	11	Paperwork
4	Controls	8	People		

PEOPLE CODING

A	Alone	E	Customer
B	With Boss	F	Others
C	With Secretary		
D	With Staff		

		8 30	9 30	10 30	11 30	12 30	1 30	2 30	3 30	4 30	5 30
MON.	ACTIVITY										
	WITH										
	INTERRUPTIONS										
TUES.	ACTIVITY										
	WITH										
	INTERRUPTIONS										
WED.	ACTIVITY										
	WITH										
	INTERRUPTIONS										
THURS.	ACTIVITY										
	WITH										
	INTERRUPTIONS										
FRI.	ACTIVITY										
	WITH										
	INTERRUPTIONS										

Each Week - Summarise and express each component of your time as a percentage of your total time

Classification of activities

PLANNING
Crystal ball gazing. Looking into the future. Using foresight. Setting objectives. Anticipating and preventing problems. Decision-making. Thinking of new strategies, new methods, new product development, cost reduction, brain storming.

ORGANISATION
Establishing lines of responsibility and authority. Assigning functions and work tasks. Defining job specification and descriptions for yourself and your subordinates. Matching people with jobs – 'horses for courses'.

CO-ORDINATION
Balancing activities, ensuring their transactions at right times, right places, right proportions. Organising Work Flow. Working out communications. Ensuring the division of labour is efficient and fair.

CONTROLS
Checking on the progress of work – seeing that objectives are being met. Setting up systems of control. Problem solving, responding to events when things go wrong.

MOTIVATION
People counselling and development. Praising and encouraging. Personnel administration. Explaining and administrating company personnel policy, benefits and salary reviews. Setting performance standards for the individual and performance appraisal. Providing rewards and taking disciplinary action. Human relations – settling disputes, problems of sickness, tardiness, etc.

ACTIVE SKILL TIME
Accountancy, selling, research, law, chemistry etc. Brain time on skill you have been trained for.

TRAVELLING
From home to office. Within work times and other journeys. Within factory or office.

MEETINGS
Business Meetings.

TELEPHONE
Time spent on telephone and the number of calls YOU deal with.

Classification of activities

UNPRODUCTIVE TIME
Doing the wrong thing, menial tasks you could have delegated. Idle time, waiting for and in meetings. Awaiting interviews. 'Hanging around' generally.

PAPERWORK
All correspondence, dictation, sorting papers, filing, cleaning desks and drawers.

TALKING
Unnecessary discussions, gossiping, passing time on pleasantries.

IS YOUR TIME PERFORMANCE LIKE THIS?

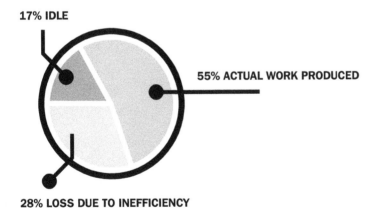

17% IDLE

55% ACTUAL WORK PRODUCED

28% LOSS DUE TO INEFFICIENCY

Express each of your activities as a percentage of your total time

A typical manager's work log may reveal the following:

Travelling	2%
Meetings	16%
Telephone	8%
Paperwork	17%
People	7%
Planning	6%
Controlling	10%
Creative	2%
Active Skill Time	17%
Talking	10%
Unproductive work	5%
	100%

Question:
Is he spending sufficient time on PLANNING, ACTIVE SKILL TIME and his PEOPLE?

Interruptions in WEEK

MONDAY	50
TUESDAY	33
WEDNESDAY	32
THURSDAY	42
FRIDAY	57
	214

Question:
If so many interruptions how can he concentrate, plan and get things done?

TIME ALONE	15%
WITH BOSS	10%
WITH SECRETARY	11%
WITH STAFF	7%
WITH CUSTOMERS	17%
WITH OTHER EMPLOYEES & OTHER PEOPLE	40%
	100%

Question:

Is he spending sufficient time with his staff?

Is he alone too little?

Is he getting the right mileage?

47

Completion of the log is simple in itself but also hard because it involves self-discipline and will power. FORCE YOURSELF, for it is the best investment you will ever make reaping priceless benefits.

The results are sure to surprise you!

READ the full section of TIME MANAGEMENT before completing your first week.

ORGANISING TIME

Start by THINKING about the key priorities and objectives you wish to achieve. Consider whether you are spending sufficient time on these so as to make significant contributions to really important things in your work and life.

This time can be termed ' discretionary time' which is available for the big tasks on which presently, perhaps, only a small proportion of your time is spent. The higher up in an organisation you are, the larger proportion of time not under your control and the greater the need to set aside huge sections of it on the management of "C.C.L.O.O.M.P."

C	CONTROLLING
C	CO-ORDINATING
L	LEADERSHIP
O	ORGANISATION
O	OBJECTIVES
M	MOTIVATION
P	PLANNING

ACTIVE SKILL TIME

So many brains go down in the drain in this country and studies of higher skilled people – doctors, chemists, engineers, lawyers – show that many of them spend too much time on work not involving the skills for which they were specifically trained. "What am I really employed to do?" is a question you must constantly ask and then ensure that you are doing it. As little as 15% of a salesman's time is actually devoted to selling in many cases. Accordingly, in improving productivity, one must endeavour to set aside huge proportions of time to make sure that these are used on your particular skill or on the areas of the work that would make a significant contribution to performance and productivity.

48

Planning your time

We all know that anything worthwhile and meaningful demands a prodigious time effort and procrastination or not organising ourselves correctly means we get nothing important done.

Start by estimating how must discretionary "BIG THINGS" time you can realistically call your own and apportion the appropriate amount you wish to spend. Three possible ways of getting this time in peace and quiet without useless distraction are:

Work at home one day a week. If you are getting results do not feel guilty about not attending the office.

Schedule regular work periods at home in the morning when your mind is fresh and you are capable of your best thinking. Thoughtful managers spend a couple of hours each morning before going to work rather than taking work home in the evening and taking twice as long to do it because they are too tired and not at their best mentally. Taking work home is a personal indictment against efficiency because it indicates you have failed to manage your time during the day.

When in your office arrange to be out at certain times and keep interruptions and the telephone away from you until 10.30am.

PLANNING YOUR TIME

Studies prove what common sense tells us that the more time we spend planning a project, the less total time is required to do it and the more successful it will be. CONCENTRATION is the name of the game and of all the principles of time management this is the most important. Concentration is CONTROLLED attention and the act of focusing the mind on a given desire until ways and means for its realisation are worked out and successfully put into operation. Success comes after much concentration. Controlled attention is thought power and the energy we can generate through the mind is a vital tool. Concentration is nothing more than being able to ignore diversions.

Give time therefore (Force yourself) to manage by anticipation and plan ahead. Set aside a little time on Sunday to roughly plan your next week mapping out an approximate schedule as overleaf. Further development and detail can be completed as following pages

Having decided where you will start and what you will do, your work planned programme should not be inflexible. Without the programme it usually means that we are not really clear in our minds how we are going to use our time. A Programme gives us direction. It keeps us working steadily and methodically and enables us to look ahead. It is also a psychological encouragement because we can tick off on our list what we have done and promote the feeling of achievement. Allocate time also for contingencies.

49

Plan your day and week

Success comes almost always to those with definite plans.

By an intelligent planning of the day's work:

You accomplish more because you have a definite quota of work assigned.

Work requiring concentration is given those hours when you are at your best.

You obtain an accurate measurement of your potential performance.

You are able to finish each task in its proper order.

You finish the day's work unhurried, unworried and almost as fresh as when the day started.

PLAN YOUR WORK AND WORK YOUR PLAN

PLANNING TIME MEANS SAVING TIME

Murphy's Law

"Left to themselves, things go from bad to worse. Anything that can go wrong will go wrong. If there is a possibility of several things going wrong, the one that will go wrong is the one that will do the most damage or if everything is going well look out because you have obviously overlooked something."

A weekly plan of work

	Monday	Tuesday	Wednesday	Planning Chart Weekly Plan
Morning	Discussion of New Project	Trip to X Factory for whole day	Next Years Budget	Desirable ideas, projects, plans. Discussion of new product.
Afternoon	Recruitment Interviews	Y Factory		Personal trip to other factory
Evening			Home with Family	Start project group

	Thursday	Friday	Saturday	With Family
Morning	Start project	Staff meeting		Evening at home Concert
Afternoon	Accountants meeting	Plan next months activities		
Evening	Social meeting	Concert		Name: Date: Week:

Schedule of activities

Date _____

Day _____

7.00am	
7.30am	
8.00am	
8.30am	
9.00am	
9.30am	
10.00am	
10.30am	
11.00am	
11.30am	
NOON	
12.30pm	
1.00pm	
1.30pm	
2.00pm	
2.30pm	
3.00pm	
3.30pm	
4.00pm	
4.30pm	
5.00pm	
5.30pm	
6.00pm	
6.30pm	
7.00pm	
7.30pm	
8.00pm	
8.30pm	
9.00pm	
9.30pm	
10.00pm	
10.30pm	
11.00pm	
11.30pm	
MIDNIGHT	

REF	THINGS TO DO	TIME DUE

CALLS TO MAKE

Commanding and controlling time

Plan your coming day by making a list of things to do in the order of their importance. This can be done last thing each night or fist thing each morning. The important thing is to get into the habit of preparing a schedule and assigning job priorities. Never work without ranking priorities.

If you want to fit everything into your day more smoothly and easily, know your commitments and bear them in mind. Have a good appointments diary and write things down in it immediately.

Get an early start by rising a quarter to a half an hour early each day. Not only do you set a good example to others by getting in early, you also have time to orientate yourself to the whole day before business actually starts.

Have good working habits – use every available minute to do odd tasks or prepare work and you will be amazed at what can be done in five minutes. Set a plan for the use of such odd times.

Be determined to delegate, use your secretary as a personal assistant. She can take a lot of the work load from you. If you do not have a secretary, delegate the more menial tasks you do to another person. Become an expert in using O.P.T. – OTHER PEOPLE'S TIME.

Endeavour to set deadlines for important activities. Keep two lists, one for urgent and one for unpleasant things that have to be done – each with a deadline.

Work on the EXCEPTION PRINCIPLE giving your people work to do and only expecting to be advised and interrupted when things are not going according to plan.

Make the fullest use of your briefcase. Organise your bag so that you know exactly where everything is. This avoids you having to search for material when it is needed.

In self-organisation, think things through and be ready to start a job with all the information on hand you will need to complete it. This will avoid you having to take time to search for something you forgot. Get into the habit of storing ideas, facts and figures and other information in a reference file. Try to prepare your notes immediately after meetings, conferences and important conversations with others. In this way, you put the facts down while still fresh in your mind. Nothing is worse than to promise your subordinate something and then forget to carry out that promise or to forget something told to you by a client or a superior.

Use the telephone, text, e-mail, voicemail and special equipment such as dictating machines to save time.

Buy time by buying books and manuals and the services of consultants to provide the additional 'know how' you need.

Handle your hardest jobs at your best hours. See if you can schedule your most difficult projects for the times that you are most alert. The routine work should be done during less productive hours at the day's end rather than the start.

Make use of your spare time. This is the time to handle those routine jobs. If a caller fails to show up, do not sit idly waiting for the next one to call. Pick up a job and start it. Read and sign mail when you are waiting for a telephone call.

Learn to read faster. Many adults will read only 200 to 250 words per minute. Experts consider that about 700 words per minutes is average for an adult and think how much more efficient you would be if you could double or treble your reading time. There are books and course that will help you to do this.

Schedule your work so that you are doing related jobs. This will help put you in the swing of things. For example, you might spend several hours dictating, or you might hold a series of advisory sessions with your subordinates.

Take occasional breaks to recharge your batteries. Organise regular holidays to regenerate fresh thinking.

Write down everything you do in a day and put question marks beside things you do not really need to do or that someone else could do.

One of the best ways of sweetening our human relations and improving our self-discipline is to make a habit of punctuality. Punctuality implies organising your day by being reasonable about the number of things you try to put into it. Also you must be careful about allowing yourself enough time to deal with business and get from place to place.

Many of us complain that we have a lot to do and that we never manage to get it all done. Sometimes thinking and worrying about it makes us weary and dispirited before we start or we try to do a bit of this and a bit of that, and end up in a muddle with nothing completed. Other times we try to do too much and become fed up with work, exhausted and discouraged. Do not expect the impossible from yourself. Like everyone else you have only one pair of hands and you can only be in one place at a time. It is better to tackle one or two things and get then done with time to spare than exhaust yourself attempting to do too much.

Be decisive and act to stop yourself from being strangled by loose ends. Get a job done as fast as possible so that you can concentrate on those tasks or creative problems that require more time.

People

You can move your dictation along by leaving blank spaces in letters which your secretary or assistant can fill in. But, be certain to let the person doing this know exactly what is expected of him or her.

Carry a work envelope or file with you at all times. When you are waiting to see someone, open the file and do whatever work is in it.

PEOPLE

AVOID THE "TALKER"

People are time consumers and time wasters. Time is precious. Impress this on your own mind and those of your staff. Rather than coming to you with a problem, encourage staff to come with it half solved or with alternative solutions so that you can give a quick decision. To help facilitate this, make sure you brief well before tasks are undertaken.

Identify and avoid garrulous people in the organisation. Talking erodes times so do not let gossip or idle chatter waste your time. Let them know that you like their company but, you would enjoy it more after office hours. Avoid the company 'friend' who wanders around visiting everyone. They are usually well liked but they can disrupt your production schedule.

If someone comes to see you, fix a time limit before your discussions commence. Politely begin the meeting by suggesting the time to deal with the matter. With salesman and longwinded nuisances stand up and they will come quickly to the point. Often saying less will shorten a meeting.

A recent study of Managing Directors indicated that none of them were alone for more than ten minutes at a time. The constant switching of attention destroys your powers of concentration.

Travel tips

If you spend much of your time travelling, it makes sense to organise this time so that some work can be done. Consider going by train rather than by plane or car. If you drive, use a pocket dictation machine for notes and reports. Use the time waiting for trains or planes to catch up on reading, to draft reports or think creatively.

AT HOME

Time can be saved at home too. Shopping can be done early or late in the day to save time and stress. Make sure that you do not watch too much television as it can erode time with little or no result. Cut down on time spent reading the newspaper – 80% of it is gossip and of little value.

Time can also be saved in the routine of household chores and Shirley Conran's "Superwomen" is an excellent and exciting present for your wife. In the Fred Taylor's book "Cheaper by the Dozen" members of the family had timetables and specific household tasks to perform.

SUPER TIME TIP

"Do the things everybody has to do, when they are not doing it".

Mark McCormach

LEARN TO SAY "NO" – SAYING "NO" IS ONE OF THE WORLD'S BEST TEACHING WORDS.

Forget popularity and recognise that we agree to many tasks because we wish to be liked. Your fears of this simple word are inside you. People respect a firm "no" rather than somebody who walks the fence. Stand in front of the mirror and practise saying "no"!

Develop hour glass eyes. Let people know politely that their time is up. Do not be afraid to say "no" to invitations to attend meetings and do things which are really unnecessary because you like to be well thought of or feel it is your duty.

MEETINGS

Too many meetings are a sign of mal-administration, so ensure they are all necessary. Hold meetings or conferences just before lunch or late in the afternoon when everybody is getting hungry and you will find everyone will speed up. Consider breakfast meetings. A well-known company in Denmark have a computerised clock programmed with each executive's hourly time rate. As the meeting proceeds the clock records, in terms of TIME and MONEY, how much the meeting is costing. You can imagine how short meetings are!

INTERRUPTIONS

NOT BEFORE 10.30 AM.

TURN OFF PHONES AT MEETINGS.

Group outgoing calls as far as possible, into one period of the day.

Get your secretary to handle 50% of the calls without discourtesy.

Be like an invisible man, make sure nobody sees you!

Scorn interruptions and distractions. Never work with your door open. Look at the TIME LOG for how many times you are interrupted and how your concentration is destroyed. This can give room for error and criminal duplication of effort.

Examine your SPAN OF CONTROL.

The idea of this is that the higher level of management you attain the smaller the number of subordinates should be responsible to you. This enables supervision of complex work without spreading your thinking over too many areas and too many people. Conversely with simple work, more people can be handled because it does not require the same attention span.

How the span of control affects organisation structure

DO NOT BE A TIME BUM.

REMEMBER:
Yesterday is a cancelled cheque.
Tomorrow is a promissory note.
Today is ready cash – use it.

QUOTE

"I would wish that every rational man should, every night when he goes to bed, ask himself these questions: What have I done today? Have I done anything that can be of use to myself or others? Have I employed my time or have I squandered it? Have I lived out the day or have I dozed it away in sloth and laziness?"

Lord Chesterfield
(Letters to his son 1754)

THE KISS OF JUDAS - GIOTTO

QUOTE

"When I see a managing Director with a span of control of twelve or more, I remind them that the Son of God could only handle eleven effectively."

Bill Reddin

58

Meetings

P.P.P.P.P. – Poor preparation and planning means pretty poor performance.

Minimise the number of meetings held and make them work. Too many are a nuisance, dangerous and a sign of mal-organisation. A camel is a horse designed by a committee.

Always circulate an agenda before a meeting and ask the attendants to prepare beforehand. Give an approximation of the time the meeting will take.

Before the talking begins fix the time limit and appoint a strong chairman who will avoid circumlocution and keep to the point. Make sure people are properly seated and at ease. Think of strategic sitting also.

Begin with the objective, make sure your staff explain themselves simply and repeatedly insist upon simplicity of expression.

Clarify your own and draw out individual contributions. Stress the positive.

Try to quantify in money terms how much it costs your company. This can be done by approximating the hourly rate of all attendants and translating this in pounds as the meeting progresses.

Do not attend meetings unless you are required and they vitally concern you.

In all things teach your staff to speak less but say more and encourage more to stop listening with their mouths.

A good time for a meeting is 11.30 when everyone wants to go for lunch or at the end of the day when they are eager to get home.

Ensure concise minutes with nominated people responsible for actions and deadlines. Sum up decisions reached.

Parkinson's Law of Meetings – "The time spent on any item on the agenda is in inverse proportion to its importance."

Effectiveness and money

Time and money are synonymous.

Most people have a mistaken impression of the economic value of their productive time – their estimate is always almost far too low. Quantifying your time in money terms and its wastage through bad utilization will make you more aware of its importance.

Time records kept be Lawyers and Accountants and billing accordingly have shown that their earnings increased by 30% to 50%. Similar exercises with Doctors considerably improved their productivity. If we were to put £ signs against our activities we would quickly be in a poisition to more readily accept the value of this human effort and the high cost of ineffectiveness.

There are 10,000 minuites in a week, half a million in a year and five million in ten years. About a third is work time. How do you use your time? ESTIMATE your hourly rate of pay and then add overheads.

In a 7 day week there are 168 hours or 10080 minutes.

Do you spend it allocated as follows:

	Hours	Minutes
SLEEP	56	3360
EAT, LEISURE, LIVING	56	3360
WORK & ASSOCIATED TIME	56	3360
		10080

Time at Work

38 hours	2300 minutes
50 hours	3000 minutes
60 hours	3600 minutes

Not many people actually give special attention to such time allocation.

T.I.P.P.Y.

TIME INVESTED SHOULD BE PROPORTIONATE TO THE POUND YIELD

Professional people compute their hourly rates by starting off with how much they would like to earn in a year. The amount is then divided by their estimated working hours (taking holidays into account).

REQUIRED INCOME
£60,000

Number of working weeks - 48

48 x 5 days x 8 hours = 1920 = £60,000 = say £32

1920

Add 100% overheads   = say £32

= £64

If the hours worked are all productive – fine.

If they are only 50% efficiently and effectively used, it shoots up to £128 per hour.

CALCULATE YOUR EARNINGS AND YOUR WORTH AND BUDGET TO OBTAIN THE HIGHEST RETURN FOR THE EFFORT INVOLVED. CHARGE YOUR TIME ACCORDINGLY.

The morning commands the day

Arnold Bennett in "How to Live for 24 Hours a Day" suggested that sleep is a habit, the more sleep you get, the more you need and the more you laze, the lazier you become. We all sleep to much and our time plan should include a rule of thumb guide to follow on this point. Certainly many managers cut short their potential achievements by sleeping and resting too much, both of which often produce a negative, lethargic and despondent approach to work. More people rust out than wear out.

A Critical factor in obtaining more time is to rise as soon as the alarm goes off in the morning. The Bible says that the morning commands the day. Getting up early allows a manager to be one step ahead all day.

Many successful people are noted for their early starts. Hannibal's armies achieved success for many years by attacking the Roman's before dawn and only when a certain Roman General realized this and attacked at night were Hannibal's series of victories reversed. Romnel, the famous German General, started work at 6.30am.

Today, many business tycoons are in their offices by 7.30 am. You are probably capable of your best thinking early in the day and, therefore, it might be best to schedule the hardest and most difficult tasks for the time of your energy peak level.

Make a plan to sleep less and do not take lie-ins, which are actually only superficial rest. Go to bed early occasionally. Live more, get more done and follow Granny's advice,

"Early to bed, early to rise, makes a man healthy, wealthy and wise".

Taking work home is a personal indictment. It means you have not managed your time during the day!

D.I.I.P.
We are all guilty of giving way to distraction, impatience, indolence and procrastination.

DISTRACTION
People interruptions has been dealt with but any form of noise, pretty girls, thoughts of getting even or psychological distractions should be continually outlawed and you should be able to recognise its effect upon concentration.

IMPATIENCE
Impatience is something that leads us to do shoddy or incomplete work and in our rush to get things done, perhaps without thinking first, we invariably take far longer to do a job. Impatience means trying to handle too many jobs at one time which only leads to chaos.

INDOLENCE
All human beings suffer from this and we are naturally lazy. We must be our own Task Master and build in 'psychological carrots' or rewards for our own achievements. Set your own targets to achieve productivity and use strong will in their attainment. If you are success give yourself a reward.

PROCRASTINATION
Procrastination as mentioned before is the thief and enemy of time. Procrastination means giving into yesterday and putting off tomorrow. We display weak will and it is usually a deep-rooted habit in all of us, which recognises self-delusion and escape. Lying to yourself keeps you from having to admit you are not a "doer". Putting off allows you to escape doing unpleasant things.

Be tough with yourself and for a few minutes everyday force yourself to do things. Decide to start changing as soon as you finish reading this and taking the first step promptly is important. Try first to do a few simple things early in the morning and you will have a feeling of exhilaration knowing that before the day is 15 minutes old you have accomplished several unpleasant tasks. Apply radical surgery immediately and cut out the cancer of procrastination. Axe anything that does not give you a feeling of accomplishment or satisfaction. If you are wasting your time in activities that bore you, divert you from your real goals or sap your energy cut them out once and for all.

Ways to avoid work

A skilled procrastinator uses the following techniques to avoid important work.

Puts it off - putting off an easy job makes it difficult.

Preparing to do it - all preparation short of actual work in the hands of a skilled procrastinator can be stretched indefinitely.

Doing something else.

Try to get someone or something to do it when you know perfectly well you should do it yourself.

Put it off until after lunch, then after tea, and then the next day.

Sleep on it.

Wait until you have a clear day.

Defer it until you feel dynamic.

Hope for better weather.

Go for a walk or go for a haircut.

Set out to clear the desk first, after all getting ready to work is almost as good as actually working and usually takes far longer.

Make yourself comfortable before you begin - thought of work would make you uncomfortable.

Search for something you need to start the job.

Go and supervise somebody.

Make phone calls.

Read some reports.

Go and discuss the problem or something with someone.

Send a circular memorandum asking other peoples' opinions.

Ask secretary to dig up more data.

Start delegating other tasks so that you can be free to concentrate.

Find something urgent to do first.

Call a meeting

Go on holiday - first handing it over to someone else.

Do it now

Procrastination is the thief and enemy of time. Of all exhortations ever heard the most important and the one which has had the most manifest benefit is the phrase "DO IT NOW".

A friend of mine has a placard on his desk which says, "RIGHT NOW IS A GOOD TIME".

How many times do we put off doing something and the anxiety and concern of not doing it generates much more wasted time, energy and worry than getting down to it immediately and getting it out of the way. I once studied a man who spent five hours putting off a job, which only took half an hour to actually do. Any psychologist will tell you that putting things off rather than doing them generates more STRESS.

Many times we are filled with guilt or regrets for not having done something. How many opportunities have been missed through failure to act promptly. Take an opportunity during the lifetime of that opportunity.

Develop the habit of PROMPT ACTION and crisp precision in getting things done. Difficult or unpleasant tasks become easier.

Getting things done take courage, develop that courage and do not be faint hearted. Be ruthless in fighting procrastination, distraction and entreaties from well-wishers to abandon your goals. Avoid fruitless pleasantries when you should be productive.

Referring to the schedule of activities sheet on page 52, COMPLETE TWO LISTS:

(a) DO IT NOW (b) JOBS TO BE DONE

Have it conveniently by you or pin it up in an obvious place and refer to it daily. Tackle the jobs that need courage and the self-discipline appropriate to a manager.

Do not go home at the end of the day until all the jobs on the list scheduled for that day have been completed.

A Lawyer I knew who was the worst communicator I had ever met achieved outstanding success by constant adherence to the phrase,

DO IT NOW

See this phrase as clearly as a stag's head against the sunset - it can have amazing results.

SEEDS OF SUCCESS: Fruitful gardening is doing what has to be done, when it has to be done, the way it ought to be done, whether you want to do it or not.

Personal Systems

To get maximum personal productivity, consider carrying out your own work-study and motion economy exercise.

If possible, use all of the latest office technology, which is increasingly available at lower costs and economically justified. Think about getting yourself a personal microcomputer and setting up your own executive workstation. Software already available can provide a 'things to do list' as well as a calendar management, which allows you to create, print and store a personalised calendar for any day, week or month now or in the future. It can also act as an electronic filing system allowing you to retrieve key information by simply indexing a word.

For saving time consider using close circuit television for meetings, holding conferences on the telephone or using CONFRAVISION.

Organise your personal systems so that you may locate the item you need immediately. Sort out keys and obtain duplicates and set up a key cupboard. Have an efficient pending file as well as one for correspondence awaiting your reply. Make sure that your filing system is good.

Have your secretary construct a personal card index system of necessary facts and have a tickler system to remind you of future important dates, i.e. payment of insurance premiums, medical checks and timetables of information due to you. A planning or white board in your office can help you to remember things as well as helping you explain points to staff. Write things down, never trust your memory.

CLEAR DESK PLAN

Many executives pile their desks high with paperwork to give the impression of hectic industry. To be organised, you need to avoid clutter, clear your desktop and work on just one matter at a time. It is psychologically bad to have books and papers heaped all over the place and it is an indictment against your personal organisation. Worse still, staff will follow your example. Have the best desk available and regularly spring clean it. Documents, files, equipment should all be in their proper places.

Microsoft Outlook is an excellent computer system to cover all of the above.

Paperwork simplification

Paperwork can strangle you and your organisation unless you keep it under control. Paperwork is a means to an end, not an end in itself. The office is the nerve centre of an organisation and, if this is efficient, it must reflect itself on the overall organisation in terms of profitability and effectiveness. Accordingly your systems, methods and procedures as well as equipment should be the very best and kept simple and effective.

Like Marks and Spencer be determined to simplify at all times and have a vendetta against paperwork. Take time regularly to examine systematically all your forms and systems and question their necessity. The key questions to ask are contained in Rudyard Kipling's wonderful little poem:

"I have six honest serving men,
They taught me all I knew,
Their names are What and Why end When,
Where and How and Who".

With correspondence, endeavour to answer all letters immediately on receipt or certainly within 24 hours. Handle letters only once. Use ready reply type letters or blitz replies (where you write straight on to a letter you have received a short note and return it to the sender keeping a photocopy for your own records) thus facilitating early action and saving on typing.

Use email, e-commerce, fax transmission methods and remember that sometimes for unimportant communication the telephone is cheaper than letters.

Ask your staff about the problems, they will soon tell you where the wheels are squeaking. Question how much can be eliminated, the methods employed and who is doing what. Question the place, possibility of duplication, when it is done. Can the method be improved, should someone less or more able do it? Can costs be reduced? Can we emulate other successful companies' administrations? Think of systems to prevent rather than make more work. Look at KEY AREAS of clerical activity and ensure internal checks and CONTROLS are satisfactory so that fraud, error and inefficiency are spotlighted.

Obtain the latest office technology for doing paperwork as it leads to greater speed, accuracy, uniformity and legibility, more control and economy as well as improved information. Taking into account tax allowances, grants and depreciation any machine probably really costs half of its original cost and, written off over its lifetime, costs far less than people. File only what is necessary and remember FILE 13 - the wastepaper basket - is a good ally. Call in, if necessary, 'Organisation and Methods' men, attend Office Equipment Exhibitions milk the brains of equipment salesmen and get free magazines like "Office Equipment News". Each day new equipment is coming out which can tremendously improve productivity. Remember there is a gold mine of cost reduction in paperwork study and a simple formula is as follows:

CUT IT OUT if it is really necessary CUT IT DOWN then FIND THE BEST METHODS and don't forget to MOTIVATE YOUR PEOPLE.

Using your time more profitably

A number of business surveys have indicated that the average manager works fifty to sixty hours a week. They take work home with them and lives with a spouse who struggles, often unsuccessfully, to keep them human.

They carry their work, often unfinished, back to the office. There, they will have one hour alone each day. The rest of the time, they are being interrupted every eight minutes by subordinates or other executives seeking advice or answers to problems. Most of these problems are things other executives are being paid to resolve.

They spend 80% of their time communicating and only 20%, doing creative work (which includes thinking)

The Chest and Heart Association say this is fatal. So set yourself some objectives, an ACTION PLAN.

1. To reduce interruptions by 50%.

2. To reduce time spent on the telephone by 50%.

3. To reduce time on correspondence by 30%.

4. To double the time spent on planning and thinking.

5. To allow half an hour every day for self-analysis and creativity.

6. To delegate properly a further 25% of your own workload.

7. To make full use of your secretary.

My action plan for better time management

Areas in which I can improve	Steps to be taken for Improvement

Qualities of a good leader

The problem has long exercised my mind as to what are the qualities conducive to good leadership, the qualities that get people "to do things they don't want to do but like it", the qualities which great leaders like Churchill, Napoleon and George Washington used in their success.

Careful analysis seems to suggest that the following factors may be the ones common to all who aspire to leadership.

They are self-confident and a positive thinker.
They are competent at what they are doing.
They have enthusiasm and the quality to inspire.
They have intelligence in a common sense way and applies their knowledge meaningfully.
They are a deep thinker, a philosopher and observer of life.
They have a sense of purpose and get results.
They show by example.
They do things rather than talk about doing things.
They exploit strengths.
They are dynamic, have energy and can go that extra mile.
They are articulate.
They have personality and a certain charisma.
They are a good decision maker.
They are robust, a survivor and can take knocks.
They are people centred, knows about human nature and obtains high productivity.
They do the right thing at the right time.

They are able to persuade and sway minds.
They are industrious and uses his imagination.
They are a true manager.

Maslow's Hierarchy of Human Needs
A Satisfied Need is No Longer a Motivator

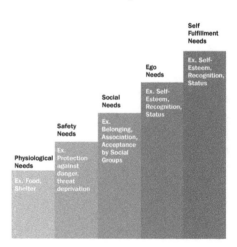

70

Getting productivity - needs of people

On a flight to Bermuda I was once sitting next to the Chairman of a very important international company. During our conversation I asked what was the key ingredient in his rise to the top. Being a Scottish chartered accountant I was expecting a reply concerned with financial astuteness but he stated without hesitation that it was his ability to handle people. The same question put to quite a number of successful people has resulted in the same answer.

It seems sensible therefore to consider what practices would lead to obtaining higher productivity and performance from your people, and which would get cooperation from workers and customers.

Many behavioural scientists have studied the situation in great depth. MacGregor set out his theories X & Y, the former that people have to be driven, and the latter that people want to work and that it is as natural as play. Maslow produced his hierarchy of human needs illustrated before. Today's guru is the American behavioural scientist Hertsberg who puts forward his motivational theory, essentially that people really wish to work, be fulfilled and do not only work for the money - although this may be a Jewish/American conspiracy to pay low wages. Any shrewd observer of obtaining productivity from people will notice that there is a lot of mileage in his philosophy and that there is no correlation between what we pay our people and their productivity because after a while no matter how highly you pay, people expect it as a right. Certainly pay your staff the best you can afford but also direct attention to their needs and quality of work life.

Simply stated these needs are for a good and secure living and a satisfactory working environment. People like to work in groups and have a sense of belonging. As individuals they need to be recognised, to know what is going on and have a chance to progress. Most of all they need something worthwhile and interesting to do - to be fulfilled and to be stretched.

As well as being aware of team spirit every good manager should know how to give his staff just that little something extra that will challenge and test them which in turn generates a good deal of satisfaction and encourages growth. We are all capable of higher accomplishments than we think. I am always surprised at the ability of people, even the most junior.

Turn your staff on (they will be twice as effective) by generating confidence in them; by example and by your ability to use their talents better than they can themselves. Constantly remember their needs for achievement, recognition, responsibility, growth, challenge and job enrichment. To achieve this delegate more, ensure participation and encourage suggestions. Staffs are crying out to be led and to be treated as people. Treat them the way you expect to be treated and practice good leadership. Remember again that good leaders get people to do what they do not want to do - and actually like it.

Have regular staff training and quality sessions.

Identify the needs and benefits of having internally run seminars. Let them study other similar organisations. Look at their academic and formal education and the possibility of sending them to college for further professional training. Make them come up with action proposals on a return from any course and make direct use of what has been learnt. You have an obligation to help your people realise their full potential and you must consider yourself a people developer and an educator.

REVIEWS & MERIT RATING

Endeavour to set up a regular review to assess and monitor performance. If you do not, you are not properly judging and recording subordinates' achievements and potential. Focus on results rather than "what kind of person he is".

Judge people on merit, not 'loyalty or yes men'. Have the courage to remove incompetents - it is always cheaper in the long run.

Have them keep their own training logbook and use this also as an error record. Do not treat mistakes as crimes but rather learning experiences and encourage discussion of causes (complexity of work, boredom, lack of knowledge) rather than blame.

SUCCESSION

Always have someone else trained to do the work of any member of staff. Do it by job rotation or swapping job knowledge and make this a definitive policy. It will save you much stress and maintain work continuity. That policy should apply to your own job and you should be proud that work goes well in your absence.

A good manager is concerned with three jobs; his own, teaching it to someone else, and then learning the job of his superior.

PATHWAYS TO PARTICIPATION

Develop your peoples' ability to see all aspects of their work and the work of the company and involve then in problem solving and decision-making. Look for their possible introduction of new ideas and a fresh view to how the work should be done.

Make sure everybody knows what he or she is doing. Ensure that people who have initiative and who like responsibility and can handle it reach the level where they can use this exceptional ability because this is talent you can never have enough of.

Awaken every possible talent and indoctrinate the drones as well as the bees.

Basic guides which can help you in working with people

The finest mnemonic in human relations end communications is:

S.I.C.R.

Keep people feeling SECURE - INVOLVE them - CONSULT them - RESPECT them.

Be grateful to your employees and you will have more to be grateful for.

REMEMBER:

COOPERATION CANNOT BE FORCED.

YOU COMMUNICATE MORE THROUGH ACTION THAN THROUGH WORDS.

SENTIMENT AND EMOTION COUNT.

LOGIC IS LIMITED.

EVERY WORKER LIKES TO FEEL IMPORTANT.

EVERYONE WANTS TO KNOW THE SIGNIFICANCE OF HIS JOB.

DON'T FORGET TO SHOW APPRECIATION FOR A JOB WELL DONE.

LEARN TO LISTEN TO PEOPLE.

BE SINCERELY INTERESTED IN YOUR EMIPLOYEES AND THEIR WELFARE.

People come in various shapes, sizes and degrees of neurosis. Handling them is the ultimate refinement of skill, so rare that it is named with typical British understatement, 'common sense'.

QUOTE

"What you would not want done to yourself, do not do unto others."

Confucius

73

People centred managers achieve results.

They know people are emotional and take things personally and that in handling them you need inexhaustible patience, an unshakeable nervous system, unfailing insight, deep wisdom and understanding, decisive judgement, in frangible physique, irrepressible spirit and an awful lot of experience.

THE SEVEN 'A's' OF MORAL BUILDING

Affection - Be affectionate and like people.

Admiration - Admire them and show respect.

Ambition - Be ambitious and expect high standards.

Activate - Be active and generate energy.

Accessibility - Talk to them and be seen.

Articulate - Tell them how they are doing.

Appreciative - Give sincere praise regularly.

A SHORT COURSE IN HUMAN RELATIONS

The six most important words are - "I admit I made a mistake"

The five most important words are - "You did a good job"

The four most important words are - "What is your opinion"

The three most important words are - "If you please"

The two most important words are - "Thank you"

The one most important word is - "We"

The least most important word is - "I"

Assertiveness

Assertive behaviour involves standing up for your own rights without violating another person's rights. It means expressing thoughts, feelings and beliefs in direct, honest and appropriate ways and is characterised by statements, which reveal that we value others and ourselves. We should want to be more assertive because it strikes a balance between aggression and non-assertion, which leads to:

Greater confidence in yourself and others.
Increased self-responsibility.
Increased self-control.
A saving in time and energy.
An increased chance of all parties meeting their needs.

The benefits of assertive behaviour in an organisation can be spotted easily. These benefits form the basis of an alternative pattern of behaviour to non-assertive or aggressive behaviour. Logically energy used up in non-assertive or aggressive behaviour could be put to better use by applying it to the real work problems.

If you do not pursue assertiveness, you generate a rat race and in the rat race the qualities that most help the individual to survive are those most likely to cause the company to fail. Like Gresham's Law bad money drives out good - with people, bad people drive out good people. The rat race implies competition within the company, which undermines co-operation between staff and their concentration on the outside world.

Look out for those who push themselves forward rather than those who push the company forward. Look out also for those managers who will not hire others better than themselves because of the threat to their own position. Reward teamwork.

Assertiveness, especially meeting different needs at once, is desirable in an organisation because it is an alternative to:

1. Managerial authoritarianism, which places more importance on the needs and rights of executives in the company rather than the organisation as a whole, including staff and workers.

2. The human relations factor, which may put emphasis on the needs and rights of the workers while neglecting the needs of the manager and the company.

Managers seek assertiveness, as a support of their beliefs that the needs and rights of their staff are important but so is their own needs and rights. Such a policy leads to company identification rather than individual or departmental identification and helps in the achievements of successful company goals.

Picking people

One of the greatest attributes of the effective manager is their skill in using the abilities of others. Many managers have harnessed this ability in their own success.

To really become effective, you must have the right people and educate and develop them. Help your people to find their true potential.

This process starts at the recruiting stage when care and effort must be taken to ensure the right selection. Good, clear job descriptions and advertisements are essential. Time and effort spent wisely here will be amply repaid later. An interview is really an investment appraisal since people are money. A secretary on £14,000 a year, employed for ten years represents an expenditure of something like £140,000 when wages and overheads are taken into consideration.

In Interviewing and recruitment thoroughness finds thoroughbreds and results in winners. Interviews should be planned to allow the interviewee to do the talking - although, of course, good talkers are not necessarily good doers, People can look and sound intelligent without being so. Prepare a rating checklist to bring system to your interviewing technique. All applicants should be tested thoroughly and verbal and written references are important. The key to what a person will do in the future is what he or she has done in the past. As basic habits rarely change, check a person's track record with care.

Ask questions about the applicant - can they actually do the job; find out about the person's skills, education, experience, intelligence, health and appearance; is there evidence of drive, energy, initiative and willingness; probe the person's stability, industry, motivation, loyalty, self - reliance, leadership qualities, likeability, maturity, perseverance and their ability to get along with others. But remember how subjective interviews can be.

When you have chosen, your responsibility has only just begun. A programme of training and education is important. The traditional learning curve reveals that people can become effective in half the normal time with a thorough and systematic training programme. Start proper training sessions, go over the job description, instigate a good induction course to introduce new people to the organisation, use a training log and try job rotation.

Rating checklist for interviewers

1 is poor; 2 is mediocre; 3 is average; 4 is excellent or considerably above average; 5 is outstanding.
Total your score below.

1. Appearance	1 2 3 4 5
2. Relevant Experience	1 2 3 4 5
3. Speech and voice	1 2 3 4 5
4. Pleasant facial expression	1 2 3 4 5
5. Likeability	1 2 3 4 5
6. Self Reliance	1 2 3 4 5
7. Sense of humour	1 2 3 4 5
8. Emotional maturity	1 2 3 4 5
9. Ability to get along with others	1 2 3 4 5
10. Articulate	1 2 3 4 5
11. Wisdom	1 2 3 4 5
12. Talkative	1 2 3 4 5
13. Technical ability	1 2 3 4 5
14. Conventionality/Stability	1 2 3 4 5
15. Fussiness/Trivia	1 2 3 4 5
16. Opinionated	1 2 3 4 5
17. Self. Educated.	1 2 3 4 5
18. Aggressiveness	1 2 3 4 5
19. Extrovert Personality	1 2 3 4 5
20. Introvert Personality	1 2 3 4 5

21. Luck	1 2 3 4 5
22. Management Ability	1 2 3 4 5
23. Well read	1 2 3 4 5
24. Perseverance	1 2 3 4 5
25. Dynamism	1 2 3 4 5
26. Leadership	1 2 3 4 5
27. Health	1 2 3 4 5
28. Industry	1 2 3 4 5
29. Qualifications	1 2 3 4 5
ABILITY TO DO THE JOB	SCORE

Interruptions management - Fort Knox

I am always surprised when managers give alibis and excuses for being constantly interrupted. Instinctively, they know that it is bad practice but, rarely do they make systematic attempts to avoid and reduce interruptions and so IMPOSE their will to control the situation.

Interruptions are kamikaze to concentration your work takes twice as long and becomes shoddy, mistakes occur, important matters are neglected and time and money are wasted. As a knowledge worker, your resource productivity is diluted and decisions are snap and of poor quality.

Interruptions management involves - PREVENTION and CONTROL.

Start out with declaring a vendetta against interruptions - TODAY. Learn to say "no". Make yourself far less accessible by getting a red "no entry" light for your door and by working with your door closed. HIDE away when doing important work.

Employ a secretary trained in a broomstick factory to screen you and take your telephone calls. Only answer and make important calls. Turn the telephone off before ten am. Ensure that getting into see you is like getting into Fort Knox.

With your people, get them to come to you always with the "solutions" to problems, rather than the problems and insist always on their recommendations. Instead of interrupting you twelve times a day, perhaps they could come to you once with twelve matters. Remember the principle of the law of •the important few

and the trivial many. Teaching staff to think for themselves will enable them to handle much of the work you previously did.

In controlling interruptions, be ruthless with your time and gracious with your people. Always ensure that they get the idea that you are doing them a favour. When you are interrupted, endeavour to set a time limit by cordial agreement.

Avoid small talk and encourage people to get to the point quickly and to keep it short. Give the interrupter your undivided attention to facilitate alacrity in dispatching business.

Keep standing and glancing at your watch. Get an hourglass or egg timer and courteously turn it over when time is up. Do not allow people to move in on your time - respect yourself.

In keeping time logs, we have always been surprised at how astounded people are at the number of interruptions they have.

You must implement a regime to prevent any unnecessary crises and interruptions so that you can have more time for the necessary ones, which you can then take in your stride.

Have that delectable feeling of achievement each day by starting now to cut down on your interruptions.

QUOTE

There is no recipe for success but, I can give you a definitive one for failure - "try to please everyone all of the time".

Selecting a secretary

A good secretary can double your worth or put you straight in front of the firing squad. Many a manager with little talent but with a certain basic charm and common sense has achieved eminence and power undreamed of by their more capable contempories by using a good secretary effectively.

She can think and act for you, anticipate your needs and actions and increase your output phenomenally.

Recruit and choose her well as it can be the most important employment decision you make. Test her thoroughly and obtain verbal references. Check also that she is compatible with your personality.

Start your working relationship off firmly and insist on work of the highest quality. At the start "treat 'em mean, keep 'em keen". Explain your work to her and how it fits in with the organisation as a whole. Make a conscious effort to delegate interesting work along with the routine jobs, thereby, using her as a personal assistant. Let her - digest key reports, keep situations under surveillance, plan meetings, make out schedules, analyse data received, answer routine correspondence, manage administrative chores and sort out more minor problems.

A good secretary can smooth the mountains of work and make you truly effective. Your efforts can aid her considerable to be a good "right-hand".

Refer to the checklist of questions to make sure she is being as useful to you as possible.

Make sure you pick the right horse for the course.

Checklist for making the best use of your secretary

1. Have you defined her job?

2. Do you keep her informed of all your appointments?

3. Do you let her monitor your calls?

(a) during interviews?
(b) all the time?

4. Do you always tell her where you are going and when you expect to be hack?

5. Do you keep her fully in the picture about your work?

6. Are you fully in the picture regarding her problems?

7. Does she have enough to do when you are away?

8. Do you tell her how she is getting on -weak and strong points?

9. Do you use her memory to supplement your own?

10. Are there routine? Letters that she could write for you?

11. Do you delegate enough to her on such items as: -

(a) circulating reports and progress chasing for them.
(b) screening routine reports for you.
(c) sorting your in basket.
(d) making tentative appointments for you.
collecting papers, etc. you will need for conferences, etc.

12. Do you delegate to the full extent of your ability?

13. Do you make the best use of the dictation machine for her?

14. In using the dictation machine, do you start with all the information she needs (e.g. number of copies)?

15. When dictating to her, do you marshal your thoughts, or keep her waiting while you meditate? (Set aside special time of day for dictation?)

16. Do you hold long conversations with visitors who pop in during dictation?

17. Has she all the facilities she needs?

18. Is her work place near enough to yours?

19. Do you distract other secretaries by talking to her in her office?

20. Do you keep appointments she makes on your behalf?

21. Do you try to avoid detaining her at meal times, etc?

Buck passing

The responsibility for developing the potential
of your people; for ensuring their optimum
productivity; for a happy environment with
superlative 'team spirit' is quite clearly yours
- DO NOT PASS THE BUCK.

Money - the creation of wealth

Some of the natural laws of money are that it is immoral not to take money from suckers, expenditure expands to meet income, and money talks - it usually says goodbye.

Most people are suckers and when it comes to the question of money we seem to envy the wealthy without realising they have it through their own efforts, their enterprise, determination and definitive money policies.

Wealthy people constantly keep a tight hold of the Privy Purse and control their cash perpetually for they are aware that it is the heartbeat of all business activity. Money flows up from the poor to the rich, from the weak to the strong and from the many to the few.

As any student and historian of wealth will tell you millionaires and wealthy people have money personalities and although some were left it, most made it on their own. They believe strongly in the work ethic and that money generates more money and that Santa Claus does not exist.

Some of their policies are worth noting:

1. Be mean and mingy and learn that this is an occupational disease of the rich. Such an attitude leads to getting value and not being a money victim. There are so many stories of wealthy people paranoiac in this respect -Paul Getty the richest man in the world had a pay phone for his guests, and Rockefeller never having given a tip to his barber. The same undoubtedly applies in a business with cost regulation and we all know that if nobody is counting nobody cares.

2. Constantly control and manage your money, keep records of its receipt and payment. Take lessons from accountants, those constipated thinkers, who keep a record in the form of a Cash Book and ledgers. This is simple but so important and it seems sensible to exert constant control. I know a friend whose wife lives so far above his income that people think they are separated.

Keep records, write things down and spend time on analysis. Budget for your expenditure and prepare a cash flow statement of receipts and payments over the next year. Only by so doing are you able to control your money and ensure its proper utilisation and planning.

3. Rich people considerably use OPM - Other Peoples Money. Shakespeare's advice to Hamlet "Never a borrower nor a lender be" was not terribly good. They know that money is a very poor store of value, that it constantly looses its purchasing power and that to combat this one needs to borrow right up to the maximum in order to invest in property and other good investments.

They are constantly aware of the ravages of inflation and plan their financial strategies in order to gain from it by choosing investments, which are a hedge. They know that the money borrowed is reducing in worth.

4. They are inveterate savers and have a rule of thumb guide that at least 25% of their earnings should be saved and ploughed back into further investments.

To avoid spending money it may be worthwhile listening to the advice of my Granny. She often repeated this as she sat astride our old oven door, when we told her she was too old to ride the range.

Ask four questions before buying anything:

1) DO YOU REALLY WANT IT?

2) DO YOU REALLY NEED IT?

3) CAN YOU AFFORD IT?

4) COULD YOU DO WITHOUT IT?

All human beings are acquisitive and throughout their lives wish to possess things. Very few purchases could escape a true answer.

84

5. They never allow themselves to be financially exploited and are never victims. They know that victims like to be liked but where money is concerned logic counts not popularity.

They make sure they have clear-cut agreements in writing and signed; they know why they are entitled to charge a price for their goods or their services; they place high values on themselves; they know how to make a profit and they have learned in the University of Life the importance of money. They pick people's brains - accountants, lawyers' and bankers' - they shop around and buy copies of WHICH magazine.

Their tax strategy is such that they ensure they legally avoid tax by forming companies, being in business on their own account or, when truly wealthy, moving to an offshore location. They seek the advice of a Jewish Tax Accountant friend of mine, Izzy Bent. Izzy is so unpopular with the Inspectors of Taxes that one said of him, "When he was circumcised, the Rabbi threw away the wrong bit".

6. When negotiating prices, if they are not succeeding they change the shape of the money, not the amount - a bigger or a smaller deposit, a longer or a shorter period. They add options either real or implicit and postpone difficult parts of an agreement for negotiation later. When they are managing companies, they very often change the negotiating team, which, usually, favours the party making the change. They know it is easier to win "at home" and pick the negotiating location accordingly

7. Money people know about quality and that when you buy on price you can never be sure you have made a good buy. It is unwise to pay too much but it is worse to pay too little. When you pay too much money that is the end of your mistakes, when you pay too little you sometimes lose everything because the cheap thing you bought is incapable of operating as you intended.

The common law of business prohibits paying a little and getting a lot. It cannot be done. As Emerson said, "The cheapest is always the dearest".

If you deal with the lowest bidder, it is well to add something for the risk you run, as the extra you have to add would usually mean that you could have bought QUALITY in the first place.

DON'T BE A MONEY SUCKER

How to be a successful entrepreneur

Successful entrepreneurs exhibit several similar characteristics:

1. They are very much concerned with MAKING MONEY. This is their classic economic goal and they do not seek a quiet life or social prestige.

2. They are generally good salesmen. They find and sell what the market wants and is prepared to pay for. When their outstanding sales ability is combined with sound financial judgement, the seeds of success are sown. Many are as concerned with cash control as with sales generation and a good definition of a successful entrepreneur is a financially articulate salesman.

They know how to double their profits in a year with little additional revenue or capital expenditure and no increase in human resources by constantly embarking on policies of:

a) Cost reduction exercises - "a pound saved is worth more than a pound earned".

b) Price increases - "price should never be based on cost but on what we can persuade the customer to pay".

(c) Increasing their turnover.

In your business, work out your personal estimate of your increased profit from:

Increasing Prices%	%
Increasing Sales%	%
Reducing Variable Costs	%
Reducing Fixed Costs	%
Extra Profit	_____

3 They are capable of speedy, objective and lateral thinking; thinking things through and looking ahead. They are willing and have the courage to take risks based on gut feeling and foresight tempered with intuition. Their success can be measured in terms of ultimate achievement against initial resources.

4 They have staying power, energy and 'stickability' and the ability to survive. They are reluctant to delegate which causes considerable frustration to support executives.

5 Their need for relaxation is not apparent as they can switch easily from business to pleasure and, indeed, business is a pleasure and a game.

6 They communicate simply and require you to do the same.

7 Successful entrepreneurs live constantly with tightened belts and shortened credit periods.

Control

Many executives are in the dark because nobody has turned the light on for them. An astute manager knows, at all times, where they have been, where they are at and where they are going. In our pursuit of effectiveness, setting up the right control mechanisms is critical.

I once flew from Bermuda to New York on a Pan American Boeing 747. The voluptuous stewardess (Ida Lushbody) offered me a drink and a visit to the flight deck. In conversation, the pilot, who looked like Gregory Peck in an admiral's uniform, asked me what my profession was. Throwing out my chest, I stated that I was an accountant - the priesthood of industry! He smiled and said that they always had an accountant on board. When he boarded his plane, he had a FLIGHT PLAN and, if he went astray from this plan, his NAVIGATION AND CONTROL instruments told him accordingly. He could then take immediate action to get back on course and avoid any dangers ahead. Wasn't that what accountant's do in business?

Every effective manager should, perhaps, be like an airline pilot with his own navigation and radar control instruments and the analogy is obvious. Consider whether you have a sufficiently good control and management information system to enable you to monitor the performance of your business, make the right decisions and take quick corrective action when things go wrong. Is all of the information available you require about your key result areas? Is the information simple, relevant, timely and designed to promote action?

In control, it is necessary to understand accounts and business finance and for this purpose you need a good accountant.

Some accountants are constipated thinkers, have the disposition of a cod, the sense of humour of a funeral director and are as cold as the summit of Everest. Someone I knew described them as being as careful as male nudists getting through a barbed wire fence.

They are trained to take a pessimistic view in an attempt never to overstate profits or worth and are motivated always by prudence. Ask them about 'cosmetic' or creative accounting especially when figures reflect on you and your need to borrow. The object here would be to prepare figures on the most optimistic basis.

Accountants are in a unique position by virtue of their access to so much information to help line-management. If you have your wits about you, you will harness this resource in your favour.

Look out for the ones with a common sense approach and who are mindful of their role as information managers. Welcome them and seek their consultation and advice because they are there specifically to help you as well as all those who need financial news, owners, shareholders, employees, tax inspectors, banks, the city and many others in our business society.

Accounting is the language of business because all our efforts must eventually be measured in terms of results and money. To enable us to understand the language it is necessary that we know about Profit and Loss Statements, Balance Sheets, Cash Flow and Management Accounting.

Accountancy is essential because we need to measure and evaluate our performance, we must know how we stand financially, we need to know our worth and we need to CONTROL THE BUSINESS.

Look out for fraud, embezzlement and 'fiddle'. Wherever there is money around, somebody wants to put their hands improperly on it and, if you do not understand accounts, it is your money they will put their hands on.

The world's greatest confidence trickster was recently tried at the Old Bailey - the judge got 10 years!

MY GRANNY BALANCING THE BOOKS

Accountancy - Pictures of the Business

Accounting is involved with decision-making and is the stuff by which information is provided so that we can make the proper decisions, exercise judgements and take action.

Too many businesses commit financial KAMEKAZE through lack of the right accountancy advice. Study, and learn to read and understand the three crucial historical statements:

THE BALANCE SHEET

The Balance Sheet is a "FINANCIAL POSITION" statement of the assets and liabilities of a business. In business money either comes in or goes out and one section of the statement shows the sources of funds - where money has come from - proprietors, loans, retained profits - the other section shows how the money has been spent mainly on fixed assets and working capital. The Balance Sheet is a capital statement where items of a permanent nature are shown.

THE PROFIT AND LOSS STATEMENT

The Profit & Loss Statement is essentially a 'RESULTS' statement. This shows the revenue from sales and then deducts how much it has cost to achieve those sales to produce a gross profit. Expenses are then deducted so as to arrive at a net profit.

This is a revenue statement where items once shown have given all benefit and will not recur. Do not mix up what goes into each statement or the wrong results will be shown. Many laymen do this.

A monthly statement should be prepared for every business and for every activity within that business.

CHANGES IN THE FINANCIAL POSITION STATEMENT

Because it is quite feasible to make a profit but have no cash, this statement is important as so many companies overtrade and go out of business because of lack of working capital. This Sources and Application of Funds Statement shows HOW the business has managed its money and is a bridge between the Balance Sheet at the start and end of the year, tracing the sources of funds and then how they have applied. It is most informative and should be studied in depth.

Learn also about Inflation Accounting and Added Value statements. Both are meaningful methods of communicating the economic reality of the organization to management and employees.

Interpretation of accounts -
spotting symptoms of inefficiency

A most valuable skill to a non-accountant is to he able to read accounts meaningfully so as to determine the financial and managerial health of a business and if necessary, to know that corrective action need be taken in respect of ineffective and lethargic performance. Get to know therefore some of the most important ratios.

They can easily be extracted from a Balance Sheet and Profit and Loss Statement and the key ones expressed as percentages or in terms of time (x 12) are:

PROFITABILITY RATIO:

$$\frac{\text{PROFIT}}{\text{CAPITAL EMPLOYED}} \quad \text{X 100}$$

What return are we making on the money invested in the business. This is the most IMPORTANT measure of performance. Is it 30% - to also cover inflation?

$$\frac{\text{PROFIT MARGINS}}{\text{SALES}} \quad \text{X 100}$$

Gross and Net Profit related to Sales.
Take these regularly and watch like a hawk - if not consistent with past ask WHY?

$$\frac{\text{NET PROFIT}}{\text{SALES}} \quad \text{X 100}$$

STOCKTURNOVER:

$$\frac{\text{AVERAGE STOCK}}{\text{COST OF SALES}} \quad \text{X 12}$$

How many times can the average stock be divided into the cost of sales. This reflects whether you have too much tied up in Stock or Work in Progress. Every £100 invested in stocks incurs 25% stockholding costs.

$$\frac{\text{W.I.P}}{\text{COST OF MANUFACTURE}}$$

DEBTORS RATIO:

$$\frac{\text{DEBTORS}}{\text{SALES}}$$

Debtors related to your sales – how long are customers taking to pay. Are customers using your money for too long and have you good credit control? Get your money as soon as it is due.

CREDITORS RATIO:

$$\frac{\text{CREDITORS @ END}}{\text{PURCHASES FOR YEAR}} \quad \text{X 12}$$

Creditors related to purchases for the year will tell you the length of time you are taking to pay your suppliers. Do not pay too quickly.

OPERATING RATIO:

$$\frac{\text{WAGES}}{\text{SALES}} \quad \text{X 100\%}$$

Related various components of Profit and Loss Statement to Sales i.e. wages, materials used, administration selling and distribution cost to Sales.

GEARING RATIO
OTHER PEOPLES MONEY
OWN MONEY

BORROWED FUNDS
SHARE CAPITAL PLUS RESERVES   Are you borrowing sufficiently? Use as much O.P.M. as possible taking into account inflation and interest rates.

WORKING CAPITAL RATIO:

CURRENT ASSETS
CURRENT LIABILITIES How do we stand for ready funds to pay our suppliers and other debt's due to be paid shortly?

QUICK ASSETS – (Debtors & Cash)
CURRENT LIABILITIES

MISCELLANEOUS:

RESEARCH
SALES   X 100
Correlation between expenditure on Research and Development and profitability.

SCRAP
COST OF MANUFACTURE
Too much waste and inefficiency.

There are many financial and operating ratios available. Search out and make sure you know well the key ones relating to your business and compare with your competitors and use them often as a means of taking action to improve profitability.

91

Management informatiom

A collective term embracing all reports, statistics, financial and operating data and other information needed by managers at all levels of an organisation to assist them In planning and decision making and to keep them informed on how well they and their subordinates are performing their assigned responsibilities.

Some factors to be considered in getting the information which Is so important to your control and performance are as follows.

All information should be presented to you:

1. In a concise and clear format and in round pounds.

2. It must be comparable with other figures, i.e. last year or budget or other peoples figures.

3. It must be useful and designed to promote action.

4. It must be timely and be news not history. Remember that sensible approximation rather than meticulous accuracy can help you to get figures far more quickly. It is far better to be sensibly approximate and have information when it can be acted upon than to have it meticulously accurate when it is far too late for action.

5. Make sure it is brief and to the point.

6. Think of economy and that the information should not cost you more to prepare than the benefit you are getting from it.

7. Make sure it is reliable, truthful, and objective. Mark Twain said that "there are good liars, bad liars and statistics".

8. As a manager you need also to consider economic intelligence about the political, economic, technological and social aspects of your work.

Ensure that in all the above you are obtaining the information from all activities within the business and these can be remembered by the mnemonic F.R.O.M.P.P.P.

FINANCE
RESEARCH AND DEVELOPMENT
ORGANISATION
MARKETING AND SALES
PEOPLE
PRODUCTION
PURCHASING

Management accounting, budgetary control and standard costing

For us to know where we are going we need to express our future objectives, plans and policies in money terms and then CONTROL them by means of a budgetary control system. This is essentially setting standards or targets for all activities and then comparing them against actual results to determine any variances. If there are any - we ask WHY - analyse the cause and subsequently take corrective action.

Arnold Weinstock once the dynamic managing director of G.E.C. spent half of his working month looking at his company's accounting ratios and actual as compared with budgeted results.

He asks the question of his executives. Have you achieved your budget? If not, why not and what are you going to do about it - FAST!

To be effective we have to be like the mafia - be quick to spot obstacles and then eliminate them.

A budget is financial or quantitative interpretation of future plans and policy to be pursued for a defined period.

A system of budgetary control is establishing budgets relating to the responsibilities of executives to the requirements of that policy and the continuous comparison of actual against budgeted results to secure by individual action the stated objectives or to provide a basis for their revision. Some call it 'People' or 'Responsibility Accounting' - and it epitomizes the exception principle.

The aims of budgetary control are to constantly plan and control all income and expenditure, capital expenditure, and ensure proper financing of adequate working capital. All this will enable you to decentralise responsibility at the same time centralising control and will allow failure to be traced to its source.

Involving all managers, set up budgets in every activity area. Then bring them all together to produce A MASTER BUDGET which will be a profit and loss statement and a balance sheet for the next year - see over.

MAKE SURE YOUR ACCOUNTING SYSTEM IS COMPUTERISED.

The master budget

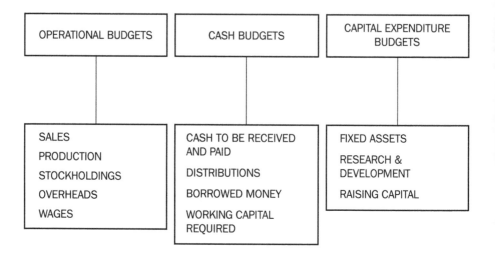

In your management information system obtain frequent statements comparing ACTUAL results against the budget and when there are variances ask the big questions...

WHY?
WHAT Happened?
WHO is responsible?
WHEN?
HOW can we put it right?

Costing - or being a cost reduction tiger

It is a truism that if nobody is counting, nobody cares and successful money people watch costs like a hawk!

Winning companies are profit and cost orientated. Therefore, know your costs and set up systems for regulating every cost within the organisation - it makes good sense. Being cost conscious will help you constantly eliminate waste and inefficiency, get value for money, cut costs, price better, reveal mistakes, know whether to eliminate waste and inefficiency, get value for money, cut costs, price better, reveal mistakes, know whether to buy in rather than manufacturing and, most importantly, make better business decisions. As a by-product, you will also have improved measurements of labour and plant utilization, material usage and accountability, stock, work in progress and overheads control.

Have regular cost reduction exercises, scrutinising all areas of cost and examining in fine detail all expenditure. There is a gold mine of cost savings in such an activity.

There are many systems available - job, process, operating, marginal but the epitome of all costing is standard costing. Here, predetermined costs are set for each product and then these are measured against actual. The differences are known as 'variances' and, by measuring labour, material and overhead variances with regard to usage, price and efficiency, we are able to direct our attention to where things are going wrong and to take quick remedial action.

Good systems of costing, standard costing and budgetary control are essential to business efficiency. If you have a good system, your company performance will be considerably improved.

The communication process

COMMUNICATIONS

"If people who do not understand each other at least understand that they do not understand each other, then they understand each other better than when, not understanding each other, they do not even understand that they do not understand each other".

Communications really means UNDERSTANDING - Getting through to people and a meeting of minds.

So much misunderstanding, calamity, aggravation, unhappiness, business failures, litigation, wasted effort and energy are the results of poor communication.

Ineffective communications is a weakness from which we all suffer. Study communications to become more aware of their importance in every day living and analyse and develop your ability.

People are not on the same wavelength as you because of barriers:

They do not listen.
They do not understand.
They and you are not concentrating.
You are speaking a different language.
You are not making yourself clear.
They have their own problems.

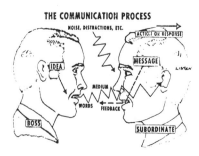

THE COMMUNICATION PROCESS

In a conversation between two people it has been said that there are six parties present:

What you say.
What the other person says.
What you think you say.
What he thinks he says.
What the other person thinks you said.
What you think he said.

Learn to speak less and say more - K.I.S.S. - Keep it simple and stupid - like the Ten Commandments or the Lords Prayer. Beware of the people who "listen with their mouths" and young and nervous people being so fearful that they are not really aware of what is being said.

Strive to always make yourself understood. What is said is often different to what is meant. What is said may be different from what is heard.

Think first then speak rather than the reverse. We think five times faster than we can talk so try not to talk too quickly.

Do you listen and really hear? Do you look and really see? Always concentrate and give attention.

For important matters give some thought to "thinking" on what you are going to communicate.

Ask the SIX relevant questions:

WHAT, WHY, HOW, WHEN, WHERE, WHO.

What am I really communicating and why? Who to?

How will I do it? When is the best time?

WRITTEN COMMUNICATIONS

Test your written communications regularly and apply the FOG INDEX method. This is to count the number of words in a sentence, the use of uncommon, complex and multi syllable words and difficulty in understanding. Use good plain words. Try writing letters, which are short and sweet.

Write in a clear and coherent manner using words with coherent and everyday meanings. Reports should be appropriately divided and captioned by sections. Consider also simplifying commercial, business policies. These might be explained better by using examples to show difficult concepts.

Can you communicate by pictures or flow charts? - Confucius he say, "One picture is worth a thousand words".

For such communications ensure that you do know what you are saying and the person who wrote, "If we really want to communicate correctly convert what we have to say into Chinese and then back again into English" had the right idea.

In verbal communications test the effectiveness of what you say by questions and PLAYBACK. Give and receive it. Have empathy with your people. Remember most people are not logical but emotional. Communicate with the heart but never listen with it.

Be a face watcher. Remember that we communicate with more than words - by a smile, touch, example and body positions. Look out for bodily signs of boredom, fear, apathy, co-operation and rebellion.

Let your people know what is happening, do not be a Bible communicator.

"Let not thy left hand know what thy right hand doeth". Mathew Ch.6 V3.

WHY PRESENT DATA IN GRAPHIC FORM

ADVANTAGES OF GRAPHIC PRESENTATION:

1. COMMUNICATES QUICKLY.

2. FORCEFUL
HAS MORE IMPACT THAN TEXT OR TABLES.

3. REVEALING.

4. CONVINCING.

5. CAN BE ATTRACTIVE.

A few rules for good communications

So much we read in every day life is a whole load of gobbledygook. Always be mindful of Peter Drucker's first rule in any good communications - what is obvious to you nobody else understands.

In all communications endeavour constantly to keep things simple. There is nothing on earth that cannot be simply explained. People who simplify place simple human values far above the claims and arrogance of experts and specialists. It takes a lot of courage to be superficial; to be an audacious simplifier who sees the fundamental currents in a sea of information and this always reflects itself in achievement.

Sometimes I think whoever writes Government forms and draftsmen of the law have a sign on their desk, which reads "if it is easy, make it harder; if it is harder, make it difficult; if it is difficult, make it impossible and if it is impossible then it is perfect.

SILENCE

Silence is a potent force in communication. One must teach oneself to listen more and hear more. Force yourself to be a compulsive listener and you will hear and observe far more of what is really happening. Use the power of silence like a persuasive salesman closing a sale and asking for an order? Try keeping your mouth shut more frequently and playing things close to your chest will enable people to know less about you especially those who are discerning.

There is an old story, which well illustrates this of a lion who ate a bull.

Feeling full and contented he lay down to rest in the long grass and a hunter walked by. The lion raised himself from his slumber and roared, whereupon the hunter shot him.

The moral of this story is of course, that if you are full of bull - keep your mouth shut.

A COMMUNICATION LESSON IN CUNNING.

A politician made a speech regarding an opponent and accused him:

His mother was a sexagenarian and he had persuaded a thirteen-year-old girl to be interested in philately.
He advocated social intercourse and asked Protestants and Jews to have Catholic views.
He had committed a piscatorial act on a boat, flying a British flag.
His nephew subscribed to a phonographic magazine.
His father died of a degenerative disease.
He was a blatant heterosexual.

The opponent lost!

Alas, (a word I only use under the stress of great emotion) many of us talk too much. Lateral thinking could be described as the sort of thinking, which is most easily recognised when it leads to simple ideas that are obvious only after they have been thought of; perhaps we could apply the same approach to our communication.

Robert Heller has written the finest book on money people -"The Common Millionaire". In it he writes:

"One clearly identifiable characteristic of the super manager is that he talks as little as possible, especially in public. This is partly because words waste time, and most men of true action are deeply, instinctively conscious of the way in which time, which is also money, runs through the fingers. They are also acutely aware that the more you say, the more you are liable to commit yourself — and commitment, unless you are exceedingly careful, also costs money. As in poker, so in business, part of the art is to keep the opposition guessing, because, like everybody else in the world, they will more often guess wrong than right."

The only person you can really communicate with and control is yourself; if you realise this, you have a considerable tactical advantage over so many people who never even get that far. Telling people is often called communicating but it usually isn't because they do not listen, do not understand, resent it or cannot or will not do it.

The result of this is that management misunderstand what the worker really wants and then tries to give it to him or the workers misunderstand what the manager wants and they do not try to do anything.

Winston Churchill was known as "Lord Heart of the Matter".

From a mountain of facts and information he could quickly determine what was important and implement action accordingly.

He never missed the wood for the trees!

Endeavour to become a "heart of the matter!' thinker.

QUOTE

"I know that you believe that you understand what I think I said. But I am not sure you realise that what you heard is not what I meant."

Public speaking

The ability to communicate orally is essential to success in business and yet many Managers are loath to speak in public and if asked would indicate that this is a thing they fear most. To persuade, to sell ideas, to impress one must acquire the skill to speak in public and know the basic guidelines.

The first is to make sure that you ENJOY it, that it is not a fearsome task but something that is a challenge and should provide pleasure. Tackle assignments to speak at every opportunity.

The key things are that one should be heard, have something worthwhile to say, engage the audience's attention and appear confident without being conceited.

Nine tenths of a talk or speech is already delivered if the speech has been properly prepared. Poor preparation and planning leads to pretty poor performance. Research your subject well, get interesting facts and statistics, use visual aids, and bring as much preparation to the subject as possible.

On developing confidence and poise, approach the matter with a positive thinking attitude. Look your audience in the eye. People want you to perform well; it is an embarrassment to them if you do not do so. If you have something worthwhile to say they want to hear it. Give yourself a pep talk before each performance, have courage and confidence and be convinced you can do it well.

Deliver your message with ENTHUSIASM, it's contagious, and in a pleasant congenial manner and begin in a friendly way with a smile. Very often people do not remember what you say but certainly they will remember how you said it. Get attention by bringing drama to your presentation, use gestures and he a bit of an actor. Modulate your voice by raising and lowering it, alter your speed of delivery and after any important point use a few seconds of silence so that the point can sink in. To make your meaning clear, endeavour to speak in pictures, for example "an accountant is as careful as a nudist getting through a barbed wire fence". Remember that most people take in 75%. of the message by their eyes and an effective presentation could be enhanced by visual aids.

Look good, have platform personality and capture your audience at once by arousing curiosity, by asking questions and by making it interesting. Use a little humour if you can, it helps tremendously.

If you have to Introduce speakers use the T.I.S. formula. State the topic, explain its importance and then name the speaker and his qualifications.

All good salesmen and actors know about A.I.D.A.

Attention - Interest - Desire - Action.

These simple principles apply equally in public speaking.

Memory

How can we improve our memory and the retention of facts is a seemingly important aspect of personal efficiency. Having a good memory will improve effectiveness.

Certainly the basic functions of memory training apply - impression, repetition and association helps us to remember things more clearly. Remembering names and important data and seeing "in burning red letters across the sky" important facts, names or telephone numbers will help us in our better use of memory.

Observe carefully - read, look and listen. Really open your eyes and see and make special concentrated efforts.

Get a clear impression of what you see, inculcate it on the mind.

By repeating facts and data, like a song you hear often, the information can be stored without conscious effort. Record knowledge on tape recorders and replay it several times.

Form associations by making a connection in your mind between new material and something which you already know. Think things through and simplify.

Use mnemonics - K.I.S.S. - Keep it simple and stupid.

Write things down, take notes, sketch pictures. Summarize a meeting, a conversation, an article, and a lecture immediately after it whilst fresh in your mind.

A good memory is no accident — it is intelligent habit and training.

FASTER READING

Most people read 200 to 300 words a minute, which with practice can be doubled with the same comprehension. A busy Manager having a lot to read must become practised in absorbing information quickly. You may do this by scanning lines rather than reading words individually, by linking paragraphs, by skimming material. Deciding beforehand what you want from a book or an article. Better still get a subordinate to prepare a synopsis of articles. Teach your staff to express themselves clearly.

Sometimes reading at the wrong time of day can hinder comprehension - important stuff read early in the day - as would poor organization of the matter.

Basically faster reading is a habit and its study very much worthwhile.

The art of negotiating

I wish I had learned earlier in life the art of negotiating. The skill could have been exploited profitably on many occasions and added considerably to wealth, wisdom and success.

The right technique is to recognise that successful negotiation should result in both parties being satisfied.

To make it more satisfactory from your point of view, know the rules well.

1. Prepare and plan. Aim high.

2. Know what is in the other person's shopping basket. Think out clearly the strategy from both negotiators' point of view.

3. If you give something away, get another benefit for it and trade options.

4. Be courteous and do not rush. Do not oversell.

5. Be calm, cut out your need to be liked and approach the situation logically.

6. Home in on common areas of agreement.

7. Always appear reasonable.

8. Never change the price, only the format.

9. Try to negotiate on your own territory and only with those with authority.

10. Remember the other person wants to feel important and respected. Consider their needs and how your ideas will help them. Make sure they get the facts and know the snags and the advantages.

11. Success with your presentation is founded upon understanding of the listener, looking at what is said and shown from his point of view and endeavouring to meet it.

12. Good ideas - no matter how sound they may be - will not stand-alone. They have to be presented attractively, clearly and persuasively. This means combining a listener based structure with presentation skills so that your whole presentation achieves its objectives.

QUOTE

"It is very tiring trying to hear what people are not telling you."

Lord Matthews

How to persuade

To persuade one must begin with a positive mental attitude and the belief that what you are trying to do is right. A powerful persuader has complete knowledge of any idea, product or point of view that they wish to put across and must completely believe in it and know that the solution is appropriate to the problem in question. They must be a character analyst and be able to determine the motives, strategy, and psychological make-up of the other person.

They must have the ability to neutralise their opponents mind making it fertile and receptive to the ideas to be placed in it. Never allow the other person to say "NO" and always get him into a "YES" frame of mind. To succeed one must have the qualities of a showman and the ability to reach into minds.

Exercise self-control when things are not going your way and do not be aggressive. Develop initiative and use imagination to create plans, which can be translated into action. Be an accurate thinker and go to the time and trouble gathering basic facts and "information" and never air opinions, which are not based upon knowledge.

Finally be persistent and determined to go that extra mile, never being put off by the word "NO" and never recognizing the word impossible. All things can be achieved and very often the word "NO" is a signal to begin a sales presentation in earnest.

Have a stock of rebuttals to offset every objection.

Acquire the habit of observation and note every word or action from the prospective buyer, every change of facial expression, and every movement and act accordingly.

MARK ANTONY

His speech to the crowd at Caesar's funeral was a superlative illustration of persuasion.

At the start they hated Caesar - at the end they loved him.

Mark Antony

Ideas

Remember it is child's play having an Idea compared with getting something done about it. Many people do not welcome ideas, especially in traditional organizations, as they feel that anything that undermines the established order of things undermines them personally and that ideas are potential crimes.

To sell your ideas you need to persuade and if you cannot succeed by sincere means try foul. Get the most hated person in the organisation to oppose it or mention the possibility of a competitor getting it first. Decide whether you want the idea accepted or credit for it. Very often you cannot have both. Suggest the idea to the most powerful man in the organisation and allow him to have the credit. Give it a warm emotional appeal.

UPSIDE DOWN THINKING

It helps your strategy if you know the tactics of others who oppose your ideas.

They will ignore it with dead silence, change the subject, see it coming and dodge, scorn it, laugh it off, praise it to death, mention that it has never been tried, prove that it is not a new idea, observe that it does not keep within the company policy, mention the cost, find a competitive idea to block it. They produce twenty reasons why it will not work and endeavour to modify it out of all existence and score technical knockouts by postponing it or by letting a committee have it.

Look out for such stratagems and you have more chance of overwhelming success.

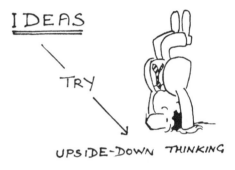

UPSIDE-DOWN THINKING

Reading people - Emotional Intelligence

People reading is a matter of opening up your senses to what is really going on and converting the insights you harvest to your advantage. Shrewd insights into people are gained simply through your powers of observation and listening and I am reluctant to admit that it was not until well into life that I discovered how tremendously important this is as a management skill. By watching and listening aggressively, by keeping eyes peeled, ears opened and mouth closed you can learn almost anything you want to know about people and in many' cases more than they would like you to know.

Learn to be a good listener. God gave us two ears - not so that we could listen in stereo but TO LISTEN MORE THAN WE SHOULD SPEAK. Some people listen so much to what they themselves are saying, they do not hear anybody else. Keep your mouth closed more often.

Consider your listen/talk ratio and just as a self-disciplined enforced five hour training session with a subordinate can give you a return on your investment of 1000 hours in saved time, more time spent listening rather than talking can pay huge dividends.

Aggressively observe by really penetratingly looking at faces, posture, eyes, dress and surroundings - all of which can reveal so much, which might otherwise go, unnoticed.

Sharpen your awareness by actively and aggressively listening and observing. Keep your antennae, radar and wits constantly about you and make it a practice, which will help you to achieve more through people and make even better judgments concerning them. In this way perhaps, we can have a slight psychological edge over others and become a little more street wise.

QUOTE

"Management is the art of getting other people to do all the work".

106

Tension and stress - the hidden handicap

Unseen by so many people are the hidden burdens, dangers and handicaps of tension and stress, which all managers have to bear. We cannot ever hope to be effective unless we are able to recognise within ourselves that tension is with us at all times and we must be able to identify it and set up a combat strategy.

Stress is nothing more than the rigours of life. A stressful manager, although technically free from illness, is unfit; his performance suffers, he worries, has palpitations, false imaginings and becomes an EMOTIONAL CRIPPLE. The stress means strain on him and handicaps efficiency and effectiveness, he is anxious and sometimes aggressive and uncertain.

Your fitness or lack of it can be measured medically in terms of your ability to tolerate stress.

Your inability to withstand stress will give rise to illness and if it occurs too quickly and frequently you are overwhelmed and give way - a heart attack, ulcers, a nervous breakdown and even cancer. Moreover you will easily become tired, joyless and angered, get headaches, bowel trouble and your common colds are more disabling.

Your enemy is of course emotional unfitness. A meeting with a superior, a hard day at the office, a quarrel, an unpopular decision, a visit from a relative, a skid, and an imminent deadline all are stresses.

Stress as a problem is really quite severe and the only solution is to cultivate an effective body and mind that is not easily overwhelmed by it.

To combat stress you must have a strategy. Set out briefly in the pages that follow are some ideas.

1. Identify it and do not be an S.S. man - Stress Sucker.

2. Learn to relax.

3. Develop a sense of humour.

4. Have a good philosophy of life because it is so short and has to be lived.

5. Have a positive mental attitude.

6. Avoid worry.

7. Be physically fit.

STRESS
BATTLE

107

The stress sucker - the burnt out syndrome

The American behavioural scientists, Freedman and Rosen, identify two types of business personalities. One who suffers great problems with stress, TYPE 'A' and the other TYPE 'B' where stress plays little part in their life style. The latter are people who are generally relaxed and uncompetitive, have no time pressures, little worry but very little ambition, and few are managers.

If you have a chronic sense of time urgency, wish to do everything perfectly, produce high quality work, waste time worrying about deadlines, are competitive, fear failure or fear looking foolish, have a low tolerance level and wish to do everything yourself - you are very definitely TYPE 'A'. You can further identify your personality if you are also impatient, use abrupt speech and gestures, eat and talk quickly, are over committed to the job and have excessive drive. You are even worse if you need to get the last word in every conversation, are always moving, walking and exercising rapidly, become enraged at traffic jams and find difficulty in standing in line without queue jumping. If you are also incapable of doing one thing at a time, find it impossible to listen to other peoples interests without interjecting your own points of view, feel guilty about doing nothing, constantly preoccupied, live by tight schedules and calendars, allow no time for contingencies, have clenched fists, nervous laugh, tightness and constant tension, you are committing emotional KAMEKAZE.

It is important to discuss your stress problem openly if you are to avoid a collision course.

Recognise that stress is caused WITHIN not without and you alone are responsible for it. YOU CREATE IT. It is not a reality but created in the mind and the most serious by-product of it is depression - one out of four people have depression and high blood pressure. If your blood pressure starts to rise 30 or 40 times a day, sooner or later it stays at that level.

Consider also that you yourself maybe a stress carrier like Typhoid Mary (immune herself) the New York waitress who spread typhoid across a city.

Write yourself a love letter

My Granny's common sense approach to self-confidence is called psycho-cybernetics in Universities. This owes more to behaviourism than psychoanalysis and is based on a theory of the brain, which likens its mechanism to that of a computer. It is the duty of the conscious mind to formulate problems, which it then presents to the subconscious; in just the same way an operator presents problems to a computer. What is all important in both cases is that the problems should be properly formulated. In other words the computer, whether human or electronic, must be correctly programmed.

The brain being vastly more complex than even the largest computer, its programming is a more difficult task. Its performance in fact can be jammed by influences, which do not affect the computer at all. One of the commonest is tension and stress, which severely inhibits mental action.

But the trickiest aspect of this mental programming lies in the personality of the programmer, for the servomechanism, invariably produces a solution in line with the picture he has of himself. Thus if he thinks he will fail, it ensures that his expectations are fulfilled. With a success prone personality the opposite is the case.

"If you think you cannot you can't,
  if you think you will fail you will fail,
  sooner or later life's battles go, not to the bigger
  or stronger man,
  but the man who thinks he can".

For a man who pictures himself as a failure, to succeed is a practical impossibility. Before he can produce successful solutions to problems he must programme himself for success by changing his self Image. This he can do by a series of mental exercises, which indicate the habits of relaxation, positive thinking and self-confidence.

Sometimes too it can straighten out the problems of a promising man who has suddenly come to a full stop. One was a salesman who made £18,000 a year in the least promising territory but failed to improve on this when promoted to the best. He pictured himself as a £18,000 a year man. Another brilliant engineer fell down in the job of a technical director because he had reached what in his own mind was the top and felt that had no further goal to strive for.

If we have negative thought patterns, a low self concept, relive past failures, low achievement drive, low perseverance and enthusiasm and are motivated by fear and lack of self confidence we need positive thinking.

A positive mental attitude

"Our life is what our thoughts make it" — Confucius.

Have you ever stopped to think why Mohammed Ali is "the greatest", why many outstanding sportsmen, actors, businessmen and successful people have actually achieved their success?

All successful people have an enthusiastic belief in themselves and not surprisingly this comes from having a POSITIVE MENTAL ATTITUDE. The way we THINK is important as thoughts make life and action follows thoughts and our most important thinking must be to have an intense belief in ourselves and in our ability to succeed.

Most assuredly we can motivate ourselves to have the confidence in believing that we can succeed in most of the things we do, if only we have the iron determination and tell ourselves and indeed force ourselves to do it. Moreover if you do not believe in yourself –no one else will! Your own positive mental attitudes can help you in all aspects of your personal effectiveness.

Norman Coussins in his book, "Anatomy of an Illness", wrote how he cured himself of a terminal illness through refusing to accept death. Recent medical research has confirmed this. Thinking can cure illness and improve mental and physical well being. American salesmen have tape cassettes with recorded programmes of building up self-confidence, which are played at the start of each day. Be a devout believer in positive thinking.

Accordingly make daily affirmations of your own confidence and your own strengths. Spotlight your talents and the things you have done successfully. Do not brood on the past and purposely remove negative thought patterns from your mind. Only you have the power over your thoughts and the ability to control most of the things you do. Think big and boldly and develop a will to win – it is too easy to be a loser and give up. In your thinking use your imagination; look out for new ideas and for the adventure of living. There are many new opportunities around us all of the time and some of your talent is probably unique. Look out for and observe the potential opportunities around. Perpetually question the past and your own attitudes? So many people seem to think that tradition is respectable but any change is suspect. Tradition is the democracy of our ancestors and if we are to progress we must change and look for new ideas.

VICTORY LOG

Keep a life record of all your successes and accomplishments. When you are down and depressed, review your records; it will boost your confidence well being and happiness.

110

Defeat

It is incredible the number of actual and attempted suicides each year. Someone said, never despair, but if you do, go on despite it. If we do not always succeed we must try and try again, rather like Robert the Bruce's spider. Develop stickability and be a monster of persistence. It is easy to give in. The most crucial test of our attitudes will be what we do in the face of adversity, rather than what we do when things are running smoothly. Successful people have an ability to fight on regardless, go that extra mile and to turn obstacles into advantages.

My Granny used to say "if you have a lemon make a lemonade". If something bad happens to you, can it be turned into something good? Every misfortune always carries with it the seed of an equivalent or greater benefit. In every adversity there is a potential for exploitation. The writer Thomas Buxton was often quoted as saying that he had the doctrine to which he owed not much, but all he ever had, namely that with ordinary talent and with extraordinary perseverance, all things are attainable.

Stickability always shows itself in success and many managers with only basic common sense have reached high positions because of it. If you can persevere and follow up tirelessly everything you do, never entertaining the idea of being put off, then you will almost always reach your goals and invariably far exceed your initial expectations.

POEM

When your world's about to fall
And your back's against the wall,
When you're facing wild retreat and utter rout;
When it seems that nought can stop it, -
All your pleas and plans can't stop it,
Get a grip upon yourself and stick it out !
Any craven fool can quit,
But men with pluck and grit
Will hold until the very final shout;
In the snarling teeth of sorrow
He will laugh and say: "Tomorrow
The luck will change...I guess,
I'll stick it out".
So you, when things go wrong,
And you think you can't last long,
That you've got to neither quit nor wait the final bout;
Smile, smile at your beholders,
Clench your teeth and square your shoulders,
And fight! You'll win if you will but stick it out'

Develop the ability to profit from the mistakes of the past and the wisdom with which to evaluate all things, as well as the self-discipline for complete mastery over yourself.

Budget your life to be at least 90

At 92, Bernard Shaw wrote a successful play and, at 91, Eamon De Valera was President of Ireland. Albert Schwitzer headed a large hospital in Africa at the age of 89 and George Burns won his first Academy Award at 80. Nowhere is it written that an ageing man must become a vegetable. Your brain will only become weak and incapable of action if you let it, just as muscles become flabby without exercise. Take the word out of your vocabulary and, instead of dreaming of that long rest in your 60s, consider a second career and plan for it in mid-life. Ask yourself what you would really like to do for a living if you could afford it.

OVERLOOKING THE OBVIOUS

Houdini, the greatest escapologist, was once nearly outwitted by a prison governor who used the simple device of an escape-proof cell. Houdini tried all his ingenuity but could not get free. A few minutes before the one-hour deadline for his escape, in desperation, he tried the door and it opened! It had not been locked in the first place.

Sometimes we create our own illusions of problems which do not exist and which are only the results of our own self-deception. Too many people are prone to assume that doors are locked against them, when the difficulty is actually a mental block.

TRANSCENDENTAL MEDITATION (T.M.)

The peace and calm we seek may come from such practices as transcendental meditation or yoga. T.M. is basically a technique of reaching the source of thought. Sitting in any comfortable position, with eyes closed, you relax and begin the meditation. The aim is to trace thoughts to their origins. Thoughts start deep inside the mind and rise to the surface where we recognise them; generally control over this process is subconscious. T.M. enables you to understand and refine this process and see how your thoughts develop. During T.M. the mind simmers down, becomes less active and you become aware of and experience a pleasant feeling of calm, orderliness and well-being. The advocates of T.M. claim that this is a state more restful than sleep and that its effects are as much mental as physical. It is really a relaxed awareness and brings about great peacefulness and serenity.

Yoga too can release nervous tension and increase energy and vitality. The stretching exercises are excellent but yoga is most famous for its relaxation exercises. The aim is to lie flat with your back on the floor and breathe very deeply, slowly relaxing each part of your body and, at the same time, emptying your mind and thinking thoughts of peace and tranquillity.

Daily affirmations

Johnson said, "The habit of looking on the best side of life is worth £1000". Feel and act cheerfully, confirm daily your strengths, your ambitions and your objectives.

THE BEST

Expect the best of yourself, your staff and those above you. Obtain the best in life you can afford - your house, holidays - and always provide the best you are capable of doing in your daily work.

FUMING AND FRETTING

Maturity involves controlling one's feelings and surely more people would do this if they realised that anger, fuming and fretting only sap their own energy and exhaust and impair our mental and physical efficiency. Seldom do we do justice to ourselves under such circumstances and we must develop the ability to be tolerant and patient even in the most provocative situations.

Lack of control means temporary insanity. The best antidote to this is to count to ten, speak slowly with your voice lowered, breathe deeply and smile.

PEACE

Develop the ability to be serene and tranquil. Follow the relaxation exhortations and always be placid and calm. Make haste slowly and note the importance of silence.

ALWAYS BE CALM AND PEACEFUL

Boredom

Act to avoid boredom; it is debilitating and psychologically unhealthy. Once you lose interest in life you are potentially shatterable and accordingly one must be prepared to take risks and look for the adventure of living.

A true barometer of intelligence is an effective happy life lived each day and each present moment of every day.

RULES

So many people adhere to rules without questioning their reason "there is no reason for it - it is policy". Question rules and when not applicable act accordingly in a common sense way. If the bureaucracy insist try the "Nelson's Eye" technique.

Become your own judge of your own conduct. Be prepared to question convention, think for yourself and never obey the rules without thinking. Each person must stand on his own feet otherwise he gets into a life of emotional servitude. The important thing is to determine for yourself which rules work and are necessary to preserve order. There are great rewards in being your own person and living your own life according to your own standards.

GUILT

Get rid of feelings of guilt and adopt your own value system. Do not feel guilty about anything, especially the past. If you believe that feeling bad or guilty will change a past or future event then you should be residing on another planet with a different reality system.

APPROVAL SEEKING

Recognise that at least 50% of the people you meet will never agree with you anyhow and therefore feeling sad about disagreements with your ideas and thoughts is a worthless task. Develop self-reliance, trust yourself and be capable of independent thinking. Your own opinions are the most important in the world and in your own self-assessment. Do not let other people's opinions affect your mode of thought.

Too many people sacrifice themselves to the opinions and predilections of others. Our need for approval is prodigious but if only we would realise that this is a psychological dead end with no great benefits accruing we would stop going around and living life in search of this need.

It is impossible to go through life without incurring a great deal of disapproval. Seeking approval is tantamount to saying your view of me is more important than my own opinion of myself.

Immunity from despair in the face of disapproval is a ticket to a lifetime of delectable personal present moment freedom. You cannot please everyone, that is the way the world works.

COMPLAINING

Never complain, other people have sufficient worries of their own and complaining never accomplishes anything. Complaining is ultimately folly and is time spent in a wasteful manner. It encourages self-pity and immobilises you.

JUSTICE TRAP

Recognise that there is no justice in life and that there must always be people better or worse, luckier or unluckier than we are. Nothing is ever fair to everybody.

Do not let lack of justice beat you and once accepting this fact move forward to positive action. Being burned up by Injustice is a foolish consistency, which is the mischievous handicap of our minds.

Avoid worry

60% of the hospital beds in this country are occupied by psychiatric patients. Tension and stress in the managerial position are enormous and much of this is due to one thing -WORRY. So many people suffer from worry but, for some reason, are ashamed to admit it. Go to a library and, astonishingly there seems to be only one decent book on the subject of worry despite its frequency as a problem and its insidious effects.

That book is Dale Carnagie's "How to Stop Worrying and Start Living" and it is packed full with common sense.

Live in day-tight compartments and forget the past, it has gone forever and there is nothing you can do about it. Remember the words of Omar Kyham;

"The moving finger having writ moves on!
Nor all your piety nor wit,
Can remove a word of it."

Live each day, putting as much as possible into that day. We all tend to look forward to things and we do not make the best of the present. Think about the future, of course, as I have said earlier, but do not worry about it.

If you are worried - and look out for subconscious worrying – then write down what you are worried about, analyse it, accept it and then consider the steps you can take to avoid it. Basically, this is problem analysis as in decision-making; find problem, get the facts, analyse them, arrive at decisions and then act. Aristotle used this technique 2000 years ago - human behaviour never changes.

Be mature and do not let little things upset you. Do not worry about things that may never happen, remember the law of averages - you could fly around the world for 40,000 years without being involved in any air accidents. Think also about how millions of pounds are made at Lloyds through people worrying about things, which never happen.

Avoid your worries by thinking and acting cheerfully. Smile, it is good for the teeth. Glumness and misery is reflected in the treatment you get from others. We are as happy as we make up our minds to be.

Do not expect gratitude and forget about getting even with people - it will cost you more than it will cost them. Count your blessings and do not let criticism upset you.

Relax, develop a simple, whole-hearted philosophy to life. Worrying does only one thing for you - gets you to an earlier grave.

All of the above is obvious yet how many times do we really systematically tackle the problem of worry.

Sense of humour

Many Americans consider reading the comic section in the daily newspaper of first priority before all the bad news. An American Managing Director I know tells himself a joke as soon as he rises each morning. This is repeated in his early meetings with his staff. His charm is irresistible. It seems to set a balance for the day.

Of all the Managers you meet those with a sense of humour seem to feel that life is beautiful and do not take themselves too seriously. They have sunshine and brilliance in their eyes and they look the youngest and seem to live the longest. It seems that the gift of laughter is a potent stimulant to good health. There is a great therapeutic value in having a sense of humour and it is unfortunate that more Doctors do not treat patients with laughing gas.

The sociology of humour is a most fascinating subject and in our judgement of people a great importance should be attached to their having a sense of humour. All great people have a deep sense of humour and it is almost a foolproof device for detecting greatness. A man who takes himself too seriously is seldom really a great man.

The happy times are when we have been able to laugh and a day without laughter is a lost day.

To avoid stress it is necessary to have a sense of humour and laugh when things are intolerable or when you least expect it. Laughter is a gift. Three cheers for the comedian and the clown. The possession of a sense of humour is a necessity for a go ahead Manager to meet the trials and tribulations of everyday work.

Have a daily joke! He who laughs, LASTS!

Your philosophy

DESIDERATA - 1692

GO PLACIDLY

AMID THE NOISE AND HASTE, AND REMEMBER WHAT PEACE THERE MAY BE IN SILENCE.

As far as possible without surrender be on good terms with all persons.

Speak your truth quietly and clearly; and listen to others, even the dull and ignorant; they too have their Story. Avoid loud and aggressive persons; they are vexations to the spirit.
If you compare yourself with others, you may become vain and bitter; for always there will be greater and lesser persons than yourself.

Enjoy your achievements as well as your plans.

Keep interested in your own career, however humble; it is a real possession in the changing fortunes of time.

Exercise caution in your business affairs; for the world is full, of trickery. But let this not blind you to what virtue there is; many persons strive for high ideals; and everywhere life is full of heroism.

Be yourself. Especially, do not feign affection. Neither be cynical about love; for in the face of all aridity and disenchantment, it is perennial as the grass.

Take kindly the counsel of the years, gracefully surrendering the things of youth.

Nurture strength of spirit to shield you in sudden misfortune. But do not distress yourself with imaginings.

Many fears are born of fatigue and loneliness.

Beyond a wholesome discipline, be gentle with yourself. You are a child of the universe, no less than the trees and the stars; you have a right to be here. And whether or not it is clear to you no doubt the universe is unfolding as it should.

Therefore be at peace with God, whatever you conceive Him to be, and whatever your labours and aspirations, in the noisy confusion of life keep peace with your soul.

With all its sham, drudgery and broken dreams, it is still a beautiful world.

Be careful. Strive to be happy.

Maturity

Maturity means basically good adjustment. The mature manager has survived the complexities of growing up and in that period of development has adjusted to life with attitudes and values that enables him to pursue a series of goals compatible with his own and society's goals. It assures his happiness as well as enables him to contribute more to life and society.

The mature manager is able to work with and for people who possess traits he dislikes. He often encounters them but learns to ignore these traits, because he knows that they cannot be changed, so he can concentrate on the job to be done rather than personalities. The ability to separate personal status and characteristics from skill and contribution to activity is not achieved quickly and comes from experience. It involves a willingness to achieve and accept ideas and skills irrespective of their origin and to see good points in the overall goal achievement. It encompasses a substantial capacity to control personal feeling and is an indication of a very good manager, philosophic and well adjusted.

Acceptance of criticism is also a mark of the mature manager. Criticism should be carefully listened to and accepted constructively even if negative which may be turned into something very positive. Mature managers encourage friendly dissension to force them to think through situations. They wish their work to be evaluated by others, know that it must come under scrutiny and they must be prepared to listen to criticisms and suggestions acknowledging them positively, whether it be personal or work.

Keep an open mind. Get things in perspective and take a "helicopter" view of yourself. Develop patience and understanding and recognise we are not right all of the time.

Live, love, learn, think, give, laugh, and try. Can you pack better advice into seven words?

QUOTE

The road to wisdom is simple to express!
You err and err and err,
but less and less and less!

119

The art of relaxation

A manager must learn to break the tensions of daily living or stress, home and work difficulties, problems and people will break them. They must learn to bend with these stresses and strains like a tree in the wind.

Learn first to relax your mind by taking time to meditate and by quietness and tranquillity.

Exercise, walk, stretch, work in the garden, play golf - because physical tiredness invites relaxation and sleep.

Know that confusion is one of the chief causes of tension, so organize your work, put first things first, one thing at a time, avoid hurry and develop a spaciousness of mind.

Observe that a smile is a symbol of relaxation, so learn not to take yourself too seriously and to laugh at yourself now and then.

You can relax in odd moments, almost anywhere you are.

Develop the habit of regular relaxation, which is the absence of all tension and effort.
Think ease and relaxation. Begin by thinking relaxation of the muscles of your eyes and your face, saying over and over: "Let go... Let go... let go and relax".

Think of yourself as free from tension as a baby.

Energy

Mark Twain stated, "The world belongs to the energetic".

Jeffrey Archer, the novelist, who made a million, lost it, and then made another million said "you can get to the very top if you have one gift, plus energy. You cannot get to the top if you have the gift and don't have energy".

Many men with energy who do not have any talent at all can get a very long way on energy alone in their particular profession or with their particular talent.

Energy is the one quality that guarantees all others. Whatever talents or abilities you have, they will not count without the vitality to use them. Successful men and women have boundless energy, stamina and 'joie de vivre'. A lot of energy is self-generated by good discipline and will power. Lack of energy comes from being bored and disinterested and, therefore, variety, making life more challenging and interesting, can help avoid feelings of lethargy and fatigue. Very often fatigue comes from disorganisation and WORRYING ABOUT WORK TO BE DONE rather than doing it. Keeping fit is obviously important but actually the mind is the body's main generator and having energy thoughts and not giving in to feelings of tiredness and forcing yourself to do something is the key to success.

As well as keeping generally fit and practising yoga techniques, try will power, deep breathing, walking, cold showers and the practice of resting before you are tired. Nurture methods of energy conservation by planning your routine and staying in one location rather than always being on the move, never standing when you can sit, never sitting when you can lie down. A systematic ten-minute cat nap at lunchtime each day - feet up - works wonders. Discover the time of day when your energy is at its peak (like early morning) and schedule your work accordingly.

Accomplishment is doing and doing demands drive. Without energy, drive, constant propulsion a person should never expect to become successful.

Fitness

The American Executives' Health Association have undertaken many studies on executives' health, well-being and longevity. Their recommendations are 20 minutes walking per day, at Least three hours physical exercises per week and ten minutes of basic stretching or jogging exercises per day. Their message is - live to be fit and be fit to live.

The executive who is physically fit scores over his less fit colleague in two ways. The positive advantages of fitness are extolled by enthusiasts as increasing alertness, vigour and giving the ability to cope with the pressures of modern executive life. Fitness also helps to protect against heart disease, which is a major killer among executives. There is no doubt among the experts that fitness can help in this way and in the United States recent research has shown that there has been a 28% decrease in heart problems which links up with a rise in the numbers keeping fit.

Not surprisingly, there are not many executives who are completely physically fit. Most have the philosophy expounded by Oscar Wilde who said that he lay down until the urge to exercise had passed. Approximately half of the men who die before they reach the age of 50 have at least partly caused their own deaths through a lack of moderation in their eating and drinking habits and their failure to look after their bodies.

What we can do to avoid such problems is a question that should be considered seriously. There is no need for over exertion, only a sensible and moderate programme of diet and exercise. Pay attention to good posture - the lazy man's way to fitness - sitting, standing and walking erect and without strain. Try to add half an inch to your height when sitting or standing. Make good posture a habit. Eat and drink in moderation. Eat light meals and avoid alcohol when there is a job to do. Being overweight is dangerous and keeping a check on your weight is good self-discipline. Reach your healthy weight and weigh yourself each week to try to maintain it. If you are not succeeding, try looking at yourself in a full-length mirror!

Try regular saunas, Turkish baths and massages. Take a daily bath or shower and, afterwards, a full body rub down with a rough towel from the top of your head to the soles of your feet. This improves circulation, which the Yogis tell us is our life force, and promotes long life. Not only will you feel better, you will look better with the consequent improvement in mental ability, energy and life enjoyment.

SOME TIPS AND RECAPS:

Get a pedal cycle.
Get a skipping rope.
Go swimming.
Walk to places instead of driving, stick to fitness goals.
Always walk up and down stairs.
Take up yoga.
Have a weekly sauna.
Don't sleep too much.
Get a suntan look good.
Take regular holidays.
Have regular medical check-ups and visit the Dentist

Fitness - isometrics

A friend of mine quotes the saying that whenever you feel like exercise you should lie down until the feeling passes. The American Commando exercises of Isometrics can lead to fitness without tremendous exertion.

Isometrics, yoga and good posture can maintain the average manager's health and fitness as well as keeping the body in trim.

Isometrics were discovered in the 1920s when scientists found that in an experiment the leg of a frog that was tied down for a time grew stronger than the free leg. The science of isometrics can be at the fingertips of every paunchy executive and flabby housewife who dreams of becoming trimmer and fitter. The technique is to firm and tone up the muscles without undue exertion by exercising the arms or legs against a solid, immovable object. The resulting tension and contraction stimulates nearly 100% of the muscular fibre as compared with a mere 50% or 60% with other methods.

Examples of exercises are to push upwards with the fingers onto the underside of a desk or to push the fist of one hand into the palm of the other. Thighs can be made firmer by standing with feet apart and pulling the thighs towards each other for six seconds, three times a day. Waistlines can be reduced with two exercises; first, you should pull your stomach towards your spine and hold it there for ten seconds, this should be done fifty times a day; another exercise is to breathe out deeply and push out

the stomach as far as possible and hold that position for one second, then breathe in and pull the stomach in as far as it will go and hold that for six seconds, this should be repeated six times a day.

Exercises can even be done in the car - with care! While driving to work, tighten your stomach muscles forcing the abdominal muscles inwards or, while at the traffic lights, grip the steering wheel tightly.

Exercise and keep yourself trim. The basic yoga exercises help both the mind and the body immensely. An hour or two of sport each week can be even more beneficial.

Take care of your body and make yourself as fit and as trim as you can. Do not worry about your shortcomings.

Ways to beat fatigue

DON'T think that you have to be tired, blaming it on the speed and strain of modern life.

DO recognise that you can lessen your tiredness by living sensibly.

DON'T think that you have to do everything that other people ask you to do and that to refuse is to be disliked.

DO recognise that you have to be selective as well as co-operative otherwise you will wear yourself out and let other people down.

DON'T think that it is lazy and a waste of time to go to bed early and to rest in the afternoon whenever you can manage it.

DO recognise that you can relax any time or anywhere, if you cultivate the habit of releasing your physical and mental tension.

DON'T think that if you had everything you wanted, life would be easier and you would feel less tired.

DO recognise that the best way to reduce tiredness and fatigue is to have a contented mind. Count your blessings and be thankful for what you have.

DON'T think that tiredness is necessarily due to overwork and an excess of responsibility.

DO recognise that work and responsibility weigh less heavily when we take care of our health.

DON'T think that the way you work is unimportant.

DO recognise the importance of delegating responsibility and cutting out unnecessary jobs.

DON'T cling to the past and old memories. Whether we like it or not, the past is behind us. Never stick to the old method if a new one is an improvement.

DO recognise that looking to the past is the way to feel old, think old and look old.

DON'T think that money and status are all that matter.

DO recognise that a lack of interest causes chronic frustration and dissatisfaction with life and that enthusiasm dispels fatigue.

Thoughts to steer by

1. Work smarter rather than harder.

2. Think BIG. Big success calls for people continually setting higher standards, constantly seeking ways to increase effectiveness, doing more with less effort and cost and being happy!

3. Think about strengths and weaknesses - judge people by their strengths not their weaknesses.

4. Remember and nurture self-discipline, be your own taskmaster - do something you do not like early in the day.

5. Keep your eye on the ball. Remember priorities and make sure you spend the right amount of time on the truly important aspects of your work.

6. Do more thinking - put your two feet on the desk more often.

7. Learn to trade minds with people.

8. Organise - do not fall into the trivia trap.

9. Learn to say "no".

10. Do not be a time bum.

11. Planning time means saving time.

12. Keep tight controls on your money and your resources.

13. Remember if you cannot increase the resource, endeavour to increase the yield.

14. Think about the lazy man's approach. Remember you are smarter than others if you realise the only person you can truly communicate with is yourself.

15. Train and add value to your people. Give a man a fish and you feed him for a day; teach a man to fish and you feed him for a lifetime.

16. Always be positive - when you get up in the morning you have two alternatives, to be happy or miserable, the former is so much easier. Remember make haste slowly.

Reading list

MANAGEMENT

'The Effective Executive' Peter Drucker.
'The Business of Winning' Robert Heller.
'The Practice of Management' Peter Drucker.
'Managers and their Jobs' Rosemary Stewart.
'Management and Machiavellian' Anthony Jay.
'How to Win the Business Battle' Eric Webster.
'In Search of Excellence' Tom Peters.
'A passion for Excellence'

POSITIVE THINKING

'Your Erroneous Zones' Edmund Daier.
'The Power of Positive Thinking' Norman Peale.
'How to stop worrying & start living' Dale Carnegie.

PUBLIC SPEAKING

'Public Speaking and Influencing Men in Business'. Dale Carnegie.

TIME

'The Effective Executive' Peter Drucker.
'Facing the Executive Challenge' Paul Carson.
'How to Get More Time to Get Everything Done' Edwin Feldman.

MONEY

'The Common Millionaire' Robert Heller.
'The Which Book of Money'

PEOPLE

The Human Side of Enterprise' McGregor.
'Human Motivation' Herzberg.
'How to Make Friends and Influence People' Dale Carnegie.
'The Managerial Grid' R Blake.

SYSTEMS

'Work Study in the Office' H. Cemach.
'Business Systems' American Systems & Procedures Association.
'How to Cut Office Costs' H. Longman.
'Paperwork Simplification' Marks & Spencer.
'The Office Supervisor' H. & M. Niles.

ACCOUNTING

'Accounting for Non Accountants' G. Mott.

THINK POSITIVE.

TIME IS MONEY

126